Hockey Haven

Hockey Haven

How Yale and Quinnipiac Made it
to the Top of the College Game

Chip Malafronte *and* Jim Shelton *of the*
New Haven Register

Copyright © 2013 by New Haven Register.

Library of Congress Control Number: 2013909605
ISBN: Hardcover 978-1-4836-4639-8
Softcover 978-1-4836-4638-1
Ebook 978-1-4836-4640-4

All rights reserved. No part of this book may be reproduced or transmitted in any form or by any means, electronic or mechanical, including photocopying, recording, or by any information storage and retrieval system, without permission in writing from the copyright owner.

Cover photos are by Peter Casolino.
Photos are by Peter Casolino, Arnold Gold, Peter Hvizdak, Mara Lavitt and
    Melanie Stengel.

This book was printed in the United States of America.

Rev. date: 06/13/2013

To order additional copies of this book, contact:
Xlibris Corporation
1-888-795-4274
www.Xlibris.com
Orders@Xlibris.com
136068

CONTENTS

Introduction 7

Chapter 1: The Year Before the Year 9

Chapter 2: Always a Hockey Town 12

Chapter 3: America's Oldest Hockey Program 17

Chapter 4: Good on the Ice, Great in the Classroom 22

Chapter 5: Building a Program from Scratch 26

Chapter 6: The Perfect Storm 32

Chapter 7: The Season 36

Chapter 8: Going in Different Directions 40

Chapter 9: The Road to Atlantic City 43

Chapter 10: The Tournament 50

Chapter 11: Party in Pittsburgh 55

Chapter 12: Game Day 60

Chapter 13: The Aftermath 65

Yale NCAA & National Championship History 83

Yale's National Championship Teams 85

INTRODUCTION

NO ONE, NOT even the most naive of tourists, will ever confuse Yale and Quinnipiac.

The Connecticut colleges, located just off the shores of Long Island Sound, are separated by seven-miles along Whitney Avenue between New Haven and Hamden. The contrasts between the two are as plain as night and day.

Yale is ivy-covered walls and tradition; a school now in its fourth century of producing world leaders and captains of industry. The ancient college, essentially, is New Haven.

Quinnipiac, established in 1929, spent most of its existence as a tiny school catering to local residents. Only recently has it realized a greater ambition. It established a law school. A medical school is on the way.

Yale, once one of the country's premier athletic powers, long ago made the choice to deprioritize sports.

Teams could still compete on a national level, but only with qualified students paying their own tuition.

At the heart of Quinnipiac's rapid expansion and desire to enter the national consciousness?

Athletics.

Yet one common thread remained: major college hockey. What transpired over the course of one season was in itself stunning and abrupt, a seismic shift of power that caught the nation by surprise.

Yale had fielded strong teams for several years after Keith Allain, a former goalie for the Bulldogs, was hired in 2006. By 2011, the school fielded what was widely considered its most talented group ever, a loaded squad with a real shot to make noise at a national level. But when Yale was bounced in the East Regional final, the national championship remained more unobtainable dream than reality—at least to those outside the locker room.

Quinnipiac was a relative newcomer to the major college hockey scene. With no national resume to speak of, the Bobcats were considered close to contending for an ECAC Hockey title but still years away from becoming a Frozen Four threat.

The ECAC preseason polls, released in September 2012, predicted a fourth-place finish for Quinnipiac; fifth-place for Yale.

By January, it was apparent the Bobcats had made a colossal leap. A sweep of Nebraska-Omaha just before New Year's Day made it 12 straight games without a loss. The streak that would extend past Valentine's Day, vaulting Quinnipiac to the No. 1 team in the national polls, and hit 21 games before being snapped.

While Quinnipiac hogged the national spotlight with its gaudy record and Hobey Baker candidate goaltender, Eric Hartzell, Yale was quietly establishing itself as a force to be reckoned with. Led by senior captain Andrew Miller, the Bulldogs were radiating talent and racking up victories.

Still, after poor performances in the ECAC semifinals two days before the NCAA field of 16 was announced, few outside of New Haven and Hamden gave either program much of a shot against the established powers.

How quickly perceptions are transformed. Over the next three weeks, one of the most monumental stories in the history of Connecticut sports played out in dramatic fashion. It proved that, for one season, the center of the college hockey universe wasn't in Boston, Denver, the Twin Cities or any other traditional outlet.

It was on a short stretch of Whitney Avenue.

CHAPTER ONE

The Year Before the Year

THE 2011-12 HOCKEY season ended unspectacularly for Yale and Quinnipiac.

The two teams both entered the ECAC Hockey tournament hoping to get hot, win the conference title and earn an automatic bid to the 16-team NCAA tournament.

Yale, the oldest college program in the nation, had been to the NCAAs in each of the past three seasons, making it to the East regional final in two of them but falling a step short of the Frozen Four, where the Bulldogs hadn't been since 1952.

They had finished sixth in the ECAC in the regular season. Winning the conference tournament—and getting back to the NCAAs for the fourth straight year—was unlikely.

Quinnipiac, despite playing in Division I for only 14 years, had rapidly ascended over the past several years, but had finished fifth in the regular season. The Bobcats hadn't been to the NCAA tournament since 2002.

The drought would last at least one more year.

Yale, facing archrival Harvard in a best-of-three ECAC quarterfinal series in Boston, won Game 1 in overtime and came tantalizingly close to winning the series in Game 2 before losing in double overtime. In Game 3, Yale was outmatched, losing 8-2 and watching its season end in embarrassing fashion.

Quinnipiac's season also ended in the ECAC quarterfinals, with a 4-0 loss to Colgate in Hamilton, N.Y.

Both teams had plenty of reasons to agonize over the lackluster endings to their seasons. Yale's season was its first since 2008 that ended shy of the NCAA tournament. Quinnipiac, despite being increasingly successful on the recruiting trail and increasingly popular in Greater New Haven, had gone a decade without an NCAA tournament bid.

Neither team had extraordinary expectations for 2012-13.

There were, however, reasons for both to have a quiet confidence.

The biggest reason for Quinnipiac and coach Rand Pecknold was Eric Hartzell, a goalie from White Bear Lake, Minn. who had caught the attention of NHL scouts and the admiration and respect of his teammates and coaches.

His personality proved no less interesting, from the easy way he talked with teammates and media to his pre-game ritual of juggling tennis balls.

"He's a different cat, that's for sure," Pecknold explained. "But everyone loves Hartzy."

Joining Hartzell as key contributors were Jeremy Langlois, twin brothers Connor and Kellen Jones, forwards Ben Arnt and Clay Harvey and defensemen Zack Currie, Zach Davies, Loren Barron and Mike Dalhuisen.

External expectations for Quinnipiac were reasonably high, but few people outside the Bobcats locker room expected them to contend for a national title.

The circumstances were similar at Yale, where the Bulldogs figured to finish in the top half of the ECAC standings, but weren't expected to make a whole lot of noise nationally.

The pieces, though, were there for Yale, particularly on offense. If the Bulldogs could solidify their goaltending situation, they could do more damage than was initially forecasted.

One of Yale's key players was senior forward Andrew Miller, a former Mr. Hockey from Michigan who spent two years with the United States Hockey League's Chicago Steel before arriving in New Haven.

By his senior year, Miller had been joined by forwards Jesse Root and Kenny Agostino, smooth-skating sophomore Tommy Fallen and talented freshman defenseman Ryan Obuchowski.

Yale's defense was considering the prospect of three freshmen as starters: 2011 Boston Bruins draft pick Rob O'Gara, Obuchowski and Mitch Witek. Goaltending would be interesting. Although senior Jeff Malcolm had logged the most minutes and saves the previous year, it was looking like senior Nick Maricic and sophomore Connor Wilson might see some serious playing time.

Expectations inside the locker rooms at Yale and Quinnipiac were lofty.

To the rest of the league, both programs were flying well under the radar. Union College had established itself as a media darling. The tiny liberal arts college in Schenectady, N.Y., a bottom feeder for most of its 20-year ECAC Hockey existence, was coming off an improbable run to the Frozen Four in Tampa.

Well-coached and oozing with talent, Union, with good reason, was the overwhelming choice to repeat in the ECAC.

Eight of the league's 12 coaches picked Union when its preseason league poll was released on Sept. 27. Three went with Cornell and one chose Harvard. Quinnipiac was selected to finish fourth, Yale fifth.

Neither had a first-place vote.

It wasn't apparent then just how much better Yale would be, and just how key Malcolm would be to the Bulldogs' success.

It wasn't apparent, either, what kind of dominant play would take place at the other end of Whitney Avenue or how the two would collide on the biggest stage possible.

CHAPTER TWO

Always a Hockey Town

THE SHOW YALE and Quinnipiac were about to put on in the 2012-13 season couldn't have come at a better time for hockey-starved, local fans.

They'd been without a pro team for more than a decade, despite a colorful history dating back to the 1920s. The departure of the last professional team, the New Haven Knights of the United Hockey League in 2002, left a deep void. That is, until hockey programs at Yale and Quinnipiac emerged with renewed vigor and accomplishment.

It would have delighted the Podoloff brothers.

The Podoloffs, Maurice and Nate, brought the New Haven Eagles of the Canadian-American League to New Haven in 1926. The Podoloffs owned the New Haven Arena at the time, so the Eagles had a place to roost from the get-go. Through the worst of the Great Depression, defenseman Norm Shay and his patriotic pucksters skated their way into the Elm City's heart.

After that, you had teams such as the Ramblers, the Tomahawks and the Nutmegs, but in 1954, the New Haven Blades made them all irrelevant. The Blades were bruisers—and they knew it.

There were Moose Lallo, Blake Ball and Kevin Morrison, brawlers all. There was the dreaded "CBS" line of Yvan Chasle, Claude Boileau and John Sherban. There were Dave Hainsworth, Ron Rohmer, Elgin McCann and Pierre Leblanc.

The team took its cue from its player-coach, the brilliant brute Don Perry.

He was a wild man, and fans loved him. Perry once instigated a full-on donnybrook in Commack, N.Y., after driving through a snowstorm, because he was upset the game hadn't been postponed. The

Blades were sent to the locker room and they refused to come back out, even when offered $100 a player.

Playing in the Eastern Hockey League, the Blades won their only title in 1956. The Arena, it should be noted, was perfect for the Blades and their fans. The place had more than 4,000 seats, but there were only 15 rows, so you were absolutely up-close and personal with all your favorite (or hated) skaters.

"I remember the first time my father came down from Canada to see me play," Blade Dave Hrechkosy told the Register in 1979. "There was a bench-clearing brawl. The New Haven fans were tearing down the wire screens and wouldn't let the opposing players return to their bench. I had a fight with Dennis Desrosiers and then I went after Pat Kelly, their coach. That's when the police arrived, complete with helmets, sticks and riot dogs. My father was petrified."

However, the Blades' final game in 1972 might have been the most memorable of all. It was Game 7 of a playoff series with the Syracuse Blazers, played at Onadaga War Memorial Arena.

The game's first fight broke out less than five minutes after the puck dropped. Leading scorer Leblanc had no skates until Perry sent someone out to a local sporting goods store. There was a bomb threat before the game.

It got worse.

Hometown referee Gordie Heagle of Syracuse decided to take some liberties while restoring order during a fight between Blades defenseman Blaine Rydman and Blazer Doug Ferguson. He punched Rydman in the face.

Naturally, the New Haven Blades would not stand idly by and watch a referee pummel a teammate. So goalie Jim Armstrong promptly tossed Heagle onto the ice and sat on his chest. Then he grabbed Heagle by the neck.

"I didn't intend to get so involved," Armstrong said years later. "But when I saw the linesman punching Rydman it left me no choice. I never actually hit him, although in some of the pictures it looked as if I did. When I grabbed him he said, 'Don't hit me,' so I just wrestled him to the ice and held him there."

The Blades lost the series, by the way. They left New Haven soon after, making way for the New Haven Nighthawks and a new generation of pro hockey.

The Nighthawks, part of the AHL, played their games at the New Haven Coliseum, which had just been built in 1972.

Theirs was a less bone-crushing style of play, compared with the Blades. They stayed in town for 20 years, thrilling their fans with a roster of illustrious personalities.

Most popular was No. 9, Tom Colley, whose jersey was the only one retired by the Nighthawks. Other standouts included Willie O'Ree, who broke the NHL's color barrier 14 years before he played in New Haven; goaltender Chico Resch, who went on to play in the NHL; and scoring champion Steve West, who had 110 points in the 1973-74 season.

Make no mistake, though. The Nighthawks could be rowdy, and so were their fans. If the old Arena had its "Zoo," taunting opposing players, the Coliseum had its "Jungle" in Section 14, near the visiting team's bench.

Still, the hockey itself was great. The Nighthawks reached the Calder Cup final four times and made the playoffs in 14 of its 20 seasons.

They even brought back Perry to coach the team, in 1981, wonder of wonders.

He still had a bit of the brawler left in him, too. Before returning to New Haven to take the job, he said, "Times have changed. You can't hit a guy over the head like you could 10 years ago. But I promise you we'll be an aggressive club. When the puck is in the corner, we'll go in and get it. And we'll hit everybody."

But even Perry couldn't stop the Coliseum's, and the Nighthawks', steady decline. Eventually, the Nighthawks couldn't even keep their name. The Ottawa Senators forced the team to become the New Haven Senators when Ottawa became New Haven's parent club. Ottawa bought the team outright after the 1992-93 season and moved it to Prince Edward Island.

Running roughly parallel to the Nighthawks' years in New Haven, Connecticut had a bigger hockey franchise to cheer for up in Hartford. The former New England Whalers took up residence at the Hartford Civic Center, starting in 1975.

The Whalers were part of the World Hockey Association until 1979, when they joined the NHL. That year, the roster was graced with the presence of a pair of legendary players at the end of their careers, Gordie Howe and Bobby Hull.

Fans throughout the state, including New Haven, soaked it in. The Whalers won their only division title in 1987, with Ron Francis, Kevin Dineen, Mike Liut and Ray Ferraro in the line-up. Time and finances weren't kind to the Whalers, however. They played their last game in Connecticut in 1997, before high-tailing it out of town.

That was the year pro hockey returned to the Elm City. It took the form of a minor league team called the Beast of New Haven, which had players such as Shane Willis, Peter Worrel, Byron Ritchie and Dwayne Hay. The Beast of New Haven was actually the former Carolina Monarchs of the AHL. In an odd twist of fate, the Monarchs had been left out in the cold when the NHL's Hartford Whalers moved south and changed its name to the Carolina Hurricanes.

New Haven saw two years of the Beast, followed by two years of the New Haven Knights of the United Hockey League. Among the Knights was North Haven native Mike Pomichter.

These days, even the Coliseum itself is gone. In its place is a parking lot.

Over the decades, more than 1,200 pro hockey players found a home in the Elm City. Some of them even stayed here after their careers, such as Hainsworth, who started a successful sporting goods company, and the late Rohmer, who was an iconic voice on local radio. There also were the local kids who grew up in the area and gained fame playing elsewhere.

In June 2012, NHL goaltender Jonathan Quick, of Hamden, took the Los Angeles Kings to their first Stanley Cup. Quick was named the Conn Smythe Trophy as playoff MVP. He also played in his first All-Star game, set a team record with 10 regular season shutouts and was a finalist for the Vezina Trophy as the league's best goalie.

Quick was far from the first NHL star from Connecticut. A generation before Quick, Cheshire's Brian Leetch was the envy of NHL defensemen, famously helping to lead the New York Rangers to the Stanley Cup in 1994—the Blueshirts' first Cup in 54 years.

Leetch spent 18 seasons in the NHL, setting the bar from defensemen with his passing prowess and stick handling skills.

Going back even further, there were the exploits of Bob McVey.

As a kid, McVey helped Hamden win the 1952 New England championship. Then he played for Harvard, where he won national titles in 1957 and 1958. His crowning achievement came two years later, when McVey was a winger on the U.S. Olympic hockey team that won a gold medal in Squaw Valley, Calif., at the height of the Cold War.

But whether it was locals who made good around the world, or guys duking it out on the ice at the old Arena, the thing New Haven hockey fans appreciated most was toughness.

"Maybe we didn't win every year, but we were always tough," Tennyson said. "The players were tough and the fans were tough. That's what made hockey beautiful here. It was a game for everyone."

In recent years, local fans have had to travel to Bridgeport, home of the Sound Tigers, or Hartford, home of the Whale, to get their pro hockey action. By the end of 2012, New Haven had been without pro hockey for a decade.

Luckily, Yale and Quinnipiac were there to fill the void.

Fans had been flocking to Yale's Ingalls Rink, known as the Yale Whale, since 1958. Attendance fluctuated over the decades, but it clearly started to spike after pro hockey left the city. In the mid-2000s, Yale had a string of 40 consecutive sellouts over three seasons, despite the fact that only one of those seasons ended in a winning record. By 2010, Yale had its first sellout of an exhibition game, during a school break.

Quinnipiac saw its attendance swell, too. The pivotal event was the construction of the TD Bank Sports Center, which opened in 2007. QU went from filling the 1,000-seat Northford Pavilion to offering a brand-new facility that could hold nearly 3,300 fans. This year, with the Bobcats in contention for a national championship, the arena saw its biggest crowds ever.

Between the two of them, Quinnipiac and Yale were putting hockey back in the forefront of the Connecticut sports landscape.

CHAPTER THREE

America's Oldest Hockey Program

YALE'S HOCKEY EXPERIENCE, although less pugilistic than the professional game in New Haven, runs even deeper.

It's a story of three periods, fittingly enough: early dominance, later decline and new determination. Along the way, there would be 117 years of hockey, punctuated with league titles, new conferences, brushes with greatness and eye-catching architecture, all before the 2013 team returned Yale to the top of the heap.

Perhaps most amazing is the way hockey has persevered at a school that prizes its football tradition so highly. This is the home of Yale Bowl and The Game, after all.

"I like to think all of our athletic teams are important to us," said Peter Salovey, Yale's incoming president, who has been going to home hockey games for decades. He usually sits near the tunnel at Ingalls Rink, so he can see players coming on and off the ice.

Salovey's appreciation for the game can be traced to his teen years in Buffalo, N.Y., he said. He attended two-thirds of Yale's home games this season, a fact that was noticed by students and student-athletes alike.

"We showed we can win a national championship while playing within Ivy League standards," Salovey said. "We did it without giving athletic scholarships, under strict guidelines on recruiting and practices, with players who are academically qualified to be students at Yale."

Richard C. Levin, Salovey's predecessor, has been going to Yale games even longer. He postponed a trip to China, in fact, so he could be at Yale's championship game this year.

During Levin's 20-year tenure as president, Yale's percentage of athletic recruits actually has dropped from 18 percent to 13 percent. Yale stays competitive, administrators said, because of its coaching staff, its academic reputation, its recently renovated training facility and its need-blind admissions process. This means Yale doesn't factor in financial need when considering a student athlete for admission and is willing to meet all financial need for incoming student athletes. It also means an athlete will not lose financial aid if he stops playing.

Historically, Yale owes a debt to another sport: tennis. Two Yale students in the 1890s, Arthur Foote and "blond-haired wonder" Malcolm Chace, had seen ice hockey in Canada and upstate New York while playing in tennis tournaments. They liked what they saw and organized a hockey team of their own back in New Haven.

It was this Foote-Chace crew that journeyed to Baltimore early in 1896 to make history. First they played the Baltimore Athletic club and lost. The next day, Feb. 1, they played Johns Hopkins in the first American intercollegiate hockey game. It was a 2-2 tie.

"Yale was there at the start, in 1896, and unlike Johns Hopkins, it is still there today," noted Daniel K. Fleschner in his 2003 book about Yale hockey, "Bulldogs on Ice."

Yale was a college hockey colossus, capturing titles in 1899, 1900 and 1902. They boasted guys such as Henry Stoddard, a future lawyer and hog farmer who scored 27 goals in 1902. A few years later you had Archer Harman, team captain in 1912 and 1913. The best man at Harman's wedding was none other than Hobey Baker.

The 1924 squad went 18-4-1, one of Yale's best years ever. Led by goalie Al Jenkins, Yale gave up only 30 goals the entire year.

The team's dominance continued through the 1930s. Five Yale men would play on the U.S. Olympic team in 1932 that won a silver medal, including John "Pleasure" Bent, Franklin Farrel and U.S. Hockey Hall of Fame member Ding Palmer. In 1934, Yale became part of the Quadrangular League, the forerunner of the Ivy League, and won the league title in 1935.

Then a figure straight out of NHL royalty came to town.

Murray Murdoch, the NHL's "Iron Man" who played in 563 consecutive games and won two Stanley Cups, the gent who was the first player drafted by the New York Rangers, took the reins of Yale hockey in 1938. He'd stay for 27 years.

He showed up at a point when Yale had uncharacteristically gone through several losing seasons. Murdoch added an immediate spark. The team won a league title during Murdoch's second year, going 11-6-4.

In all, his Yale squads had 15 winning seasons, brought home two league titles and made one trip to the NCAA tournament. Among the legion of Yale players during Murdoch's tenure were goalie Harrison Holt, future Olympian Fred Pearson (who wore a bright red flannel shirt to tryouts so he'd be noticed), Minnesota North Stars exec Gordon Ritz, Hamden's Ted Shay, future IBM exec John Akers, defenseman Steve Ripley and future U.S. Secretary of State Cyrus Vance.

The early 1950s was a particularly sweet period. Yale had a 32-10-1 stretch over two seasons, ending with the 1952 NCAA tournament. When Murdoch retired in 1965, he'd notched 278 wins.

By then, he had his guys playing in Ingalls Rink, known affectionately as the "Yale Whale." It took roughly three years to build and opened on Dec. 4, 1958. The great Finnish architect and Yale graduate Eero Saarinen, famous for his wondrous Gateway Arch in St. Louis, envisioned Yale's ice palace with a grand, curving ceiling that looked like the backbone of a leviathan. It was named for a pair of Yale hockey captains, David S. Ingalls Sr. (Class of 1920) and David S. Ingalls Jr. (Class of 1956).

Yet despite its edgy new digs, the program was headed for hibernation.

The late 1960s and early 1970s were a low point. Winning seasons were scarce. Crazy as it sounds, Yale hockey was waiting for someone from Harvard to shake it out of its doldrums. Enter Tim Taylor, in 1976.

Taylor was a no-nonsense guy in his mid-30s who'd been intensely involved in the sport his whole life. Not only was he from Boston, but he'd captained the 1963 ECAC champion Harvard squad and spent seven seasons as an assistant coach there. Now here he was, unpacking his bags at the Yale Whale.

"It was a struggle to keep attitudes up that first year and breathe new life into the program," he told the Register in 2001. "Clearly, my first couple of years here we were at the very bottom."

His first game was at Pennsylvania, where Yale won 3-2.

"I have vivid memories of that win," Taylor recalled. "A freshman, Gary Lawrence, a future captain and Rhodes Scholar got the winning goal and Keith Allain . . . was the goaltender. We went to Princeton the next night and lost in overtime."

After a bracing start, Taylor's Bulldogs gradually improved. By 1981, Taylor's first recruiting class won the Ivy League title. It would keep getting better.

Taylor had a remarkable run in the mid-1980s, with 19 wins in the 1984-85 season, and 20 the next year. The 1985 squad won the Ivy League crown and the 1986 crew reached the ECAC finals, losing to Cornell in double overtime at the Boston Garden. Yale was blessed with future NHL players Bob Kudelski, Randy Wood and Bob Logan.

Through it all, Taylor kept his standards consistently high, whether he was religiously analyzing film or working with players.

In the 1990s, he and Yale experienced more glory. Taylor achieved a personal dream when he coached Team USA in the 1994 Olympics; he and Yale reached a new plateau in 1998, when the Bulldogs won a school-record 23 games, an Ivy League title and their first NCAA tournament bid in 46 years. Yale had a Hobey Baker finalist that year, Ray Giroux.

"Clearly, that was an absolute highlight of my years here at Yale," Taylor said in 2001. "The accomplishments of that team exceeded anyone's expectations."

But then, in the space of a few short years, Yale hockey stumbled badly. The team lost games in bunches, and for the first time in years attendance was dropping. Alumni were not pleased, and Taylor took much of the blame.

For three years in the mid-2000s, Yale lost 19 or more games each season. The Bulldogs were 37 games below .500 during that stretch, in fact. It would be Taylor's undoing as coach. Although he'd wanted to stay with the program, he was forced to resign.

Taylor left in 2006 with more wins, 337, than any Yale hockey coach, even the great Murdoch.

So who do you bring in to revamp a venerable program? In this case, it was the freshman kid Taylor put in as goalie during that first game back in 1976—Keith Allain.

The final group of candidates to succeed Taylor included Holy Cross coach Paul Pearl, Harvard assistant Sean McCann and Dartmouth assistant Dave Peters. But they chose Allain, the goaltending coach for the NHL St. Louis Blues, who also had international coaching experience with USA Hockey.

Where Taylor was a strict student of the sport, Allain was about the fun of competition. He preferred shorter, higher-intensity practices. He wanted his players to be decisive and cast off the negative aura that had enveloped the team in recent years.

"I've always had fun with the game," Allain said in 2010, when the Register named him its Sports Person of the Year. "As a player, I was passionate about winning and losing, but I think at the same time, I liked coming to the rink. It's fun to compete, and I want our guys to feel that."

Allain's players got the message. They won Yale's first ECAC tournament title in 2009 and went to the NCAA tournament for the first time in more than a decade. The next year, they ended the season ranked fifth in the nation and were one victory away from reaching the Frozen Four.

In 2011, all Yale did was have its best season ever—or so it thought.

This was a finely-tuned machine, this squad. Yale was ranked No. 1 in the country by the middle of January. It racked up 28 wins, led by senior scorers Broc Little and Denny Kearney, talented freshman Andrew Miller, senior Chris Cahill, junior Brian O'Neill, Ryan Rondeau in goal and team captain Jimmy Martin. Only at the end, when Minnesota-Duluth tripped them up 5-3 en route to a national championship, did Yale stumble.

It was heady stuff, such acclaim and high-stakes action. The only thing more fun for Allain's team would be a national championship of its own.

CHAPTER FOUR

Good on the Ice, Great in the Classroom

THOUGH SCHOOLS IN each athletic conference face their own challenges on the recruiting trail, none compare to those encountered by coaches in the Ivy League.

In many ways, the toughest challenge for an Ivy League athlete is being accepted into the school.

The Academic Index, a formula that takes into account a student-athlete's high school grades and standardized test score, is every bit as important as points scored and a goaltender's save percentage. Each Ivy League administration is keenly aware of the 'AI' for every player admitted to a rival school.

Recruiting, though, is made even more difficult because Ivy League schools offer no athletic scholarships.

New financial aid policies have helped make Ivy schools more affordable to the middle class. Schools are now allowed to devote more resources to assist families that in the past would never have considered the Ivies because of the hefty price tag.

While Ivy League hockey schools always recruited well—New England prep schools have long been a hotbed—the creative financial aid packages further leveled the playing field against full scholarship programs.

Yet even with more money to assist with tuition, academic standards simply can't be compromised at Yale. So Keith Allain and his assistant coaches remain relatively limited with whom they can realistically recruit. Battles for qualified hockey players between the Ivy League schools are cutthroat and highly competitive.

When Allain was hired in 2006, he initiated a new recruiting strategy. Rather than wait on an official Academic Index score to begin the process, Yale would target younger players with strong academic backgrounds. It was a calculated risk. Academic skills needed to develop at the same rate as hockey skills. But earlier involvement would be vital in winning recruiting battles against scholarship schools as well as fellow Ivies.

"We got burned on a couple of kids because they didn't get admitted," said Kyle Wallack, Allain's top assistant at Yale from 2006-11. "You're up front with the families because it's not a done deal. But you say we'll support them as long as they do X, Y and Z and get their SATs up and keep developing."

Allain, upon his arrival in New Haven, had the benefit of two blue-chip recruits procured by his predecessor, longtime Yale coach Tim Taylor. Allain retained C.J. Marottolo, Taylor's associate head coach, and Marottolo helped snag Connecticut natives and prep school stars Sean Backman and Mark Arcobello for the fall of 2006. The pair would become building blocks for the Bulldogs' program.

Two more vibrant play-makers—Broc Little and Denny Kearney—along with charismatic defenseman Jimmy Martin, led another strong class the following year. Forward Brian O'Neill was secured to enroll in 2008, a freshman on what would be Yale's first NCAA tournament team in 11 years—a string of four berths in five years to be capped with the ultimate prize.

The school's strict admissions guidelines weeded out most of the prototypical NHL-sized players sought by heavyweights in the Midwest and Hockey East. Yale's recruiting philosophy was simple. Find competitors and proven winners. Once in New Haven, the coaching staff blended them together to find the right formula.

The common thread, it turned out, was size. More accurately, a lack of size.

"We weren't going to get the 6-foot-4 Rick Nash, Chris Pronger-type player so we went undersized and it worked," said Wallack. "Let's take the 5-8 kid. If he's fast and competitive, he's going to get to the puck first. If we get the puck, we're on offense."

Winning certainly perked the interest of prospective recruits. Bolstered by its newfound success, Yale's roster for the 2012-13 season began to take shape in the winter of 2006 during a recruiting trip to suburban Detroit.

Andrew Miller was the top high school player in Michigan. His Cranbrook Kingswood team was coached by Yale alum Andy Weidenbach. His talent was evident. Wallack watched Miller go end-to-end for a goal on the game's first shift. His potential was unlimited; good enough attend any school in the country. But Miller was also intent on a world-class education. Yale was where he wanted to be.

Kenny Agostino was a 5 feet, 4 inch sophomore at New Jersey's Delbarton School when Yale took notice of his electrifying talent. By the time he graduated, he was a three-time state player of the year and had blossomed to a 6-foot-1, 200-pound specimen taken by Pittsburgh in the NHL Entry Draft.

Some made bigger first impressions with their minds. Defenseman Colin Dueck's grades were off the charts; forward Charles Orzetti's SAT score was in the 99th percentile. Both developed into valuable cogs on the ice.

Jesse Root, a Pittsburgh native and cousin of NFL legend Dan Marino, was recruited out of Connecticut's Taft prep school with modest expectations only to become the team's top-line center.

As Yale proved it was no flash in the pan on the national hockey scene, it began to win more battles with big-name scholarship schools. Defenseman Tommy Fallen, who grew up a die-hard Minnesota Gophers fan, chose Yale's Bulldogs over the more hockey reputable Bulldogs of Minnesota-Duluth.

Miller, who got two years of post-high school seasoning in the United States Hockey League, developed into the nation's best forward. Michigan State tried to pry him away at the last minute, but he remained firm for Yale.

As Yale's hockey profile skyrocketed, it still lost every recruiting battle to an old nemesis. Harvard had beaten out the Bulldogs time and time again for talent. On multiple occasions Yale thought it finally had the upper hand over the Crimson, only for prospective players to phone the hockey office a week later with news they'd changed their minds and opted for Harvard instead.

Through it all, though, Yale had far more successes than failures.

In September 2008, Marottolo flew out to British Columbia on a recruiting trip. He hoped to secure high-scoring forward Conor Morrison for Yale. Morrison was indeed dynamic, a perfect fit for the Bulldogs' high-octane offensive attack. Yet it was the goaltender for the opposition, a player well off Yale's radar, who really caught Marottolo's attention.

Morrison, as if keeping with tradition, chose Harvard. But Yale landed the goalie. In time, Morrison's career fizzled, with just eight points over his final two seasons in Cambridge. The goalie, a lanky 19-year old named Jeff Malcolm, would become one of the most successful players in Yale history.

CHAPTER FIVE

Building a Program from Scratch

QUINNIPIAC WAS A tiny commuter college when John Lahey was appointed president in 1987. The school's intimate size and bucolic campus setting in the shadow of Sleeping Giant mountain in Hamden led to a nickname among students and visitors alike: Camp QC.

Lahey, who had been executive vice president and chief operating officer at Marist College, had a vision to expand Quinnipiac's presence beyond Greater New Haven.

He established the Quinnipiac poll in 1988, a small endeavor that began in conjunction with a marketing class and soon expanded into a nationally-recognized operation. But the real key was athletics. Lahey said he felt the truly great academic institutions all had Division I programs, and that elevating would be the best path to raising Quinnipiac's profile.

The administration targeted basketball, lacrosse and ice hockey as the sports best-suited as a vehicle for national exposure. All three could attract national and international students. All three would tie into the desired marketing and brand strategy. Quinnipiac wanted name recognition. It wanted to carve a place for itself among the country's top colleges. Attracting a stronger population of students would lead to a higher academic profile.

Quinnipiac's emphasis was on three sports, for which it would obtain the maximum amount of scholarships, the best coaches and the best facilities.

But if the school wanted a real return on its investment, the key was hockey. A niche sport that thrived in certain pockets of the country, hockey provided legitimate opportunity for much smaller schools to be successful.

It was a sport in which a previously unknown university like Lake Superior State could win multiple national championships; where an athletic program like Colorado College, Division III in all other sports, was among the most feared members of the nation's most competitive hockey league; where otherwise anonymous schools Ferris State and Alaska-Fairbanks were conference mates with the likes of Notre Dame, Michigan and Ohio State.

To envision Quinnipiac basketball at the same level as Michigan State, Wisconsin or even UConn is a pipe dream. But in hockey, with a limited number of programs and a sea of unclaimed talent for the taking, the climb from obscurity to the top of the mountain was very realistic.

There are close to 350 Division I basketball programs, but only 59 Division I hockey teams. There's an old joke in hockey: win two games on any given weekend and you're nationally ranked.

Lahey had a vision. The next step was finding an athletic director to guide the program to the next level.

Jack McDonald had extensive experience in Division I sports. He was a track star at Boston College and later worked marketing the school's athletic program. As the athletic director at the University of Denver in the early 1990s, he helped lay the groundwork for a return to full-time Division I status.

More importantly, McDonald, the oldest of 11 children in a Braintree, Mass. family, understood the importance of hockey. A brother, Gerry, played in the NHL for the Hartford Whalers. At Denver, he helped restore a once-proud men's hockey tradition from mediocrity. He hired George Gwozdecky, who would go on to win a pair of national titles.

Lahey felt McDonald, with his experience and ambition, was the perfect choice to usher in the Division I era at Quinnipiac. McDonald was excited to sink his teeth in and build for the future.

"When I interviewed in April 1995, John had mentioned his goal of going to Division I," McDonald said. "I said, 'Let's do it.'"

For all his enthusiasm and ambition, it didn't take long for McDonald to see he faced quite a challenge. He arrived in the fall of 1995 for his first Quinnipiac hockey game just before game time. It was scheduled for 9:30 on a Sunday night at the Hamden High School rink. An open public skate session was still in session.

The game started 30 minutes late. Afterward, players from both teams were forced to share the only locker room with a working shower.

"I thought 'What the heck did I get myself into?'" McDonald said.

One crucial component McDonald inherited was a young hockey coach with a drive as fiery as his head of red hair. Rand Pecknold, just 26, was hired a year earlier by the previous athletic director, Burt Kahn. He walked into the interview and was greeted not only by Kahn, but by his big, leaping pet dogs.

Pecknold, a New Hampshire native and former star defenseman at Connecticut College, was searching for a job as an assistant at a Division I program when he landed at Quinnipiac.

He made $6,700 his first season. Then again, the job was part-time. He taught high school an hour's drive from Hamden to make ends meet. He had 12 goalies at his first practice, forced to ask if some of them could play out. Practices were at midnight. He slept in three-hour shifts between teaching and coaching.

"I had friends ask, 'Why Quinnipiac?'" Pecknold said shortly after he was hired in May 1994. "Well, I started thinking to myself how kids I'd go after would fall in love with the campus, and how President Lahey was committed to improving the program. I knew there was a future here under those circumstances."

McDonald immediately connected with Pecknold.

"I could see that he was good and a little crazy," McDonald said. "He was young, which was key, he was well-educated, he had a great mentor at Conn College in Doug Roberts and he was an aggressive recruiter."

The pieces were in place at Quinnipiac: a school president who understood the value of big-time athletics; an athletic director convinced the school could be a hockey power; a charismatic and knowledgeable coach.

Things would move quickly. Within a year of McDonald's hiring, Quinnipiac announced its commitment to elevate its athletic program from Division II status in the fall of 1998. In hockey, it banded with several other regional schools to join a new hockey league using the name of an existing conference—the Metro Atlantic Athletic Conference.

The MAAC soon became Atlantic Hockey. Plans were drawn up for a brand new athletic complex atop newly purchased land atop York Hill that would be the centerpiece Quinnipiac's ambitious expansion plan. The complex would be state-of-the-art—a two-headed building with a standalone hockey arena and a standalone basketball arena under one roof.

Then, a real window of opportunity arose.

In 2004, Vermont accepted an invitation to join Hockey East, leaving a vacancy in ECAC Hockey. Not only could Quinnipiac join a major college hockey conference, allowing it to increase scholarships and strength of schedule, but it would rub elbows some of the most elite academic universities in the world. Quinnipiac would be directly associated with Harvard, Yale, Princeton, Cornell, Brown, Dartmouth and Colgate.

"It's all about recognition potential," said Brian Jones, a professor of marketing and advertising at Quinnipiac. "Hockey is something (school administrators) thought we could be good at, and with just 58 teams it would be relatively easy to stand out. In marketing, brand and brand equity is everything. You strive to achieve a certain image. What better way than to join the ECAC?"

Holy Cross was interested as well. Well established academically and athletically, it fit the ECAC profile to a tee. But Quinnipiac had a pair of aces in the hole.

One was the new arena, which would to replace Northford Ice Pavilion, a community rink a couple towns over that the school had used for several years.

The other was Yale.

The ancient Ivy League school had supported other Quinnipiac endeavors such as its law school and medical school. But in hockey there was little to gain and lots to lose with Quinnipiac in the ECAC.

Still, Yale threw its support behind Quinnipiac. Former Yale coach Tim Taylor, among the most respected hockey coaches in the country, at any level, was particularly adamant.

"We like the support it had from the president of the school all the way down," said Wayne Dean, Yale's senior associate athletic director and the chairman of the league's expansion committee. "We knew they'd be a great fit. The TD Bank Center certainly helped, but it was a combination of many things."

Yale's generosity went as far as granting permission for Quinnipiac to use Ingalls Rink whenever possible until the TD Bank Sports Center was completed. The Northford Pavilion had limited seating; Yale's rink provided a 3,500-capacity facility.

"If not for Yale, the ECAC would not have accepted us and we certainly would not have been in Pittsburgh for the Frozen Four," Lahey said. "Yale has long been a great friend to us, and we owe them all the thanks in the world."

The campus had always aided Quinnipiac in its recruiting efforts, but quaint surroundings and limited hockey potential only went so far. A new building and membership in the ECAC had its benefits.

The TD Bank Sports Center, opened in 2007, cost $52 million to build. Part of the cost was subsidized with a 10-year naming rights deal. That contract expires in three years. Quinnipiac stands to gain a hefty rate increase in its new negotiations.

A magnificent viewing facility for basketball and hockey, there's much more than meets the eye. The University Club offers fine dining and a full bar with windows and viewing decks overlooking each arena. There's a strength and conditioning center; an athletic training room, team study and lounge areas and pro-style locker rooms and changing rooms for both men's and women's hockey.

When the University of North Dakota first unveiled opulent Englestad Arena, with its 11,000 leather seats, imported Italian tile and multi-million dollar weight room, recruits would commit on the spot.

At Quinnipiac, skeptical recruits from the Midwestern U.S. or Western Canada who'd never heard of the school were instantly smitten. A gorgeous campus, strong academics and first-rate hockey facilities quickly puts any unease to rest.

Goaltender Eric Hartzell grew up in White Bear Lake, Minn., where every mite hockey player dreams of playing for either the University of Minnesota or its rival across the Red River, North Dakota. Hartzell's father, Kevin, won a national championship in 1979 playing for legendary Gopher coach Herb Brooks, who famously coached the U.S. Olympic team to its Miracle on Ice gold medal in 1980 at Lake Placid.

Eric had drawn some interest from North Dakota. Yet he knew he'd found a home on his official visit to Hamden.

"I loved it. I loved everything about the place," Hartzell said. "From the players and coaches to the campus to Sleeping Giant. I loved it. It would have been pretty cool to go to North Dakota, but I'm extremely satisfied."

Pecknold also managed to produce winning team after winning team, no matter how steep the transition.

Quinnipiac teams, playing a Division II/III schedule, had fewer than nine wins for five successive seasons prior to Pecknold's hiring. The team went 6-15-1 in his first season. By year four, they were 19-3-1. In the first season at the Division I level, the Bobcats went 26-6-2 and won the MAAC championship. A year later, they won 27 games. Of course, the schedules those seasons didn't feature a single opponent from one of the four major conferences.

"No one would play us," Pecknold said.

The bump to ECAC Hockey was also smooth. Quinnipiac won 20 games in its inaugural season. A year later, behind All-American defenseman Reid Cashman, the Bobcats advanced all the way to the ECAC's championship game and even took a two-goal, third-period lead over Clarkson with an automatic bid to the NCAA tournament on the line. Clarkson, loaded with NHL draft picks, rallied to win.

Quinnipiac's remarkable 2012-13 run made it 17 straight without a losing season under Pecknold.

The school went years without a player who'd been drafted by the NHL. Cashman was one of the first to develop into a legitimate prospect while at Quinnipiac. The 2012-13 roster, though, featured eight highly sought-after players. There were three to five more in the recruiting class for the next fall.

And just one day after losing to Yale in the national championship game, Hartzell signed a lucrative contract with the Pittsburgh Penguins. He'd report directly to the big club, becoming the first Quinnipiac player to make an NHL roster.

Quinnipiac's investment was paying off. When Lahey arrived in 1987, enrollment was 1,902 students, 65 percent of whom were from Connecticut. By 2012, the student body of 8,500 included 76 percent from out of state.

As the hockey team reached the No. 1 ranking in the national polls in 2013, the admissions department saw a noticeable jump in applications. Applications were up 5 percent from the previous year, meaning 21,000 high school seniors applied for the 1,800 available seats for the class of 2017.

Camp QC has come a long way.

CHAPTER SIX

The Perfect Storm

RECRUITING HAS ALWAYS been one of Rand Pecknold's strengths. Long before the sparkling TD Bank Sports Center was constructed in 2007, when his teams skated in cramped community rinks, Pecknold convinced talented players who'd never even heard of the school before that Quinnipiac was the right place for them.

In Quinnipiac's first season at the Division I level, with limited hockey scholarships, four top players from the United States Hockey League were already in tow. Among them was Long Island native Chris Cerrella, who remains Quinnipiac's all-time leading scorer.

As more money was ear-marked for scholarships, it became obvious to Pecknold that he needed to tap into Canadian Junior 'A' leagues. Ontario was a relatively easy drive. But there was an army of unclaimed talent in the Western provinces of Alberta, Saskatchewan and British Columbia.

His recruiting budget was microscopic. Yet Pecknold managed to establish a foothold for Quinnipiac in Western Canada during the late 1990s. Good fortune helped make it possible. His parents had moved to Bellingham, Wash., an hour's drive from Vancouver. An uncle lived in Surrey, B.C., in the heart of the talent-rich British Columbia Hockey League.

For the price of a round-trip plane ticket, Pecknold could stay with family and spend extensive time scouting the region. All the ambitious, young coach had to do was persuade players to travel 3,000 miles across the continent and help build a program from scratch at his tiny school with the funny sounding name.

Pecknold proved to be an able salesman.

Among the first long distance recruits was Dan Ennis, a linebacker-sized defenseman who arrived in Hamden in 1999 from the remote coastal city of Kitimat, B.C. Trips from Quinnipiac's campus to Ennis' hometown required an international flight to Vancouver followed by a 20-hour drive north. A year later, another budding star of the early days, Ryan Olson, committed from his Merritt, B.C. squad.

Many of the program's top players ever—Brian Herbert, Jamie Holden, Matt Erhart, Ben Nelson, Bryan Leitch, Brandon Wong, Scott Zurevinski—have come from the British Columbia Hockey League. Young players listening to the recruiting pitch heard stories of the successes of former BCHL players in Hamden. Visits to the pretty campus often sealed the deal.

"It just snowballed," Pecknold said. "Once you start getting great players from an area, it helps you get more great players. Over the last dozen or so years, we've had 33 players from British Columbia. My understanding is no other college program has even come close to that number."

True to form, Quinnipiac's roster for the 2012-2013 season included 14 players from Canadian Junior 'A' leagues—nine from the BCHL.

Arguably the biggest recruiting haul in program history came when a set of identical twins from Trail, B.C., a three hour drive north from Spokane, Wash., selected Quinnipiac over a slew of major college offers.

Ben Syer, then Pecknold's top assistant coach, first came across Kellen and Connor Jones as 16-year-olds playing for their Vernon, B.C. Junior team. They were small, but fearless. And they knew each other on the ice so well, it seemed like they played with extra sensory perception.

"Ben called me about these twins on the fourth line in Vernon," Pecknold recalled. "He said 'You'll love them. We're going to be all over them.'"

Over the next 18 months, the Joneses helped Vernon to consecutive Royal Bank Cups, a tournament to determine the Canadian national champions. Their profile in the small world of NCAA hockey recruiting grew exponentially. More schools took notice. The twins were so besieged by the barrage of coaches beating down their door that they stopped talking to them altogether. Letters, emails and phone calls went unreciprocated.

Syer entered Pecknold's office one afternoon to announce he had good news and bad news.

"The bad news is I can't get them to call me back," Syer said. "The good news is they aren't calling anyone back."

A handful of colleges backed off by the perceived snub. Pecknold was certain the pair was merely overwhelmed. He trekked out to their hometown to scout the pair at a game and meet the family, including the twins' grandfather, Terry Jones Sr., a one-time New York Rangers prospect who'd spent time with the old New Haven Blades. In an unprecedented maneuver, the twins were invited to visit Quinnipiac along with another prospect, Zurevinski, their line mate with the Vernon Vipers.

Zurevinski committed. The Jones twins soon followed. With them in the program, Quinnipiac's future as a national power began to take shape.

"Not just the fact that they're good players, but they improved our hockey culture with their work ethic in practice and in the weight room," Pecknold said. "They're winners."

A year later, Quinnipiac assistant coach Bill Riga phoned Pecknold from a showcase event in Ottawa to tell him about a dynamic forward named Matthew Peca. Quinnipiac had one scholarship left for its 2011 recruiting class. Riga insisted it had to be spent on Peca, just 17.

"He's a game changer," Riga told Pecknold.

Pecknold drove nine hours to watch a summer league game near Peca's hometown of Petawawa, Ontario, and drove home the next morning. It was a gesture that stuck with Peca, who picked Quinnipiac in September. By March, Peca was the outstanding player for a Pembroke club that won the Royal Bank Cup.

In time, Quinnipiac's line of Peca and the Jones twins would become one of the best in college hockey.

Other pieces of the roster were already in place; talent secured by the persistence of the Quinnipiac staff.

Pecknold watched Eric Hartzell during a practice session at a United States Hockey League showcase. He left convinced the athletic son of a coach—he played for his father, Kevin Hartzell, at Sioux Falls (S.D.)—was a future NHL goaltender. Hartzell didn't make much of an impression on other coaches when he struggled during the next day's game. Pecknold was the first to offer a scholarship. Hartzell had grown up dreaming of leading the University of North Dakota to a national championship. But his shot would come with Quinnipiac.

Forward Russell Goodman signed a national letter of intent to play for Colorado College, contingent upon his grades. When he got a 'C' in one class, the school dropped him. He landed at Quinnipiac.

Jeremy Langlois, one of the few Division I recruits from Arizona, whittled his college choices down to Boston College, Boston University,

New Hampshire and Quinnipiac. The three Hockey East powers felt he needed another year of seasoning in Junior 'A' hockey; Pecknold wanted him right away. Langlois accepted. He would finish as a member of Quinnipiac's exclusive 100-point club.

Jordan Samuels-Thomas, the lone Connecticut native on the roster, was playing in the United States Hockey League when offered a scholarship by Pecknold. UMass was also very interested.

"I thought we were going to get him," Pecknold said. "But at the last second, he said he was going to Bowling Green."

But after two seasons at the Ohio school, Samuels-Thomas was ready to transfer. Quinnipiac, a 30 minute drive from his West Hartford home, was at the top of his list.

Kevin Bui and Cory Hibbeler were both considering Division III schools before Quinnipiac entered the picture at the 11th hour. Bui eventually developed into one of the program's best clutch scorers. Hibbeler thought he'd be relegated to small-college lacrosse before Pecknold offered a spot as a preferred walk-on. So luminous was his locker room presence, he was voted team captain in April 2013.

Recruiting in general is quirky and unique. There's no rhyme or reason sometimes. Every team targets certain types of players, hoping to follow a pre-established mold. The key is the ability to deviate from the plan and the willingness to adapt.

A successful program can mold a winner under any circumstances. Since 1997, Pecknold had produced 16 successive teams without a losing record.

By the fall of 2012, he had painstakingly constructed a national juggernaut.

CHAPTER SEVEN

The Season

QUINNIPIAC'S MAIN HURDLE prior to the 2012-13 season was getting its players—and coach—securely in the barn.

Hartzell, whose skills had become scary good and were only going to get better, was a given. He'd started 27 games in goal as a sophomore, and as a junior, he set a single-season school record with a 2.20 goals against average. That put him at No. 16 in the country among all NCAA Division 1 schools.

At 6 foot 4 and 190 lbs., Hartzell had the size, technique, mental preparedness and athleticism sought by NHL programs. In the months ahead, dozens of scouts and NHL representatives would come out to see him, including Philadelphia Flyers General Manager Paul Holmgren and New York Rangers special assistant Mark Messier.

A new guy at Quinnipiac, junior transfer Jordan Samuels-Thomas, also looked promising. The 6-foot-3 Winnipeg Jets draft pick, who had led Bowling Green in scoring two years earlier, had a potential spot on the Bobcats' second line. "Jordan will score," Pecknold promised. "He's an impact kid. It's different than adding an 18- or 19-year-old freshman. He is game ready, and should be ready to contribute right out of the gate."

But then there was a trio of players talented enough to leave for the pros: forward Matthew Peca and twin brothers Connor and Kellen Jones.

Peca, a sophomore from Ontario, had been named to the ECAC's All-Rookie Team the previous year. He'd also led the team in assists and came up big in the postseason against Brown, with five points in three games. The Jones twins, forwards from British Columbia, would be juniors. They'd been named co-most valuable players the year before, and their hockey resumes included playing in the RBC Cup National

Championship in 2009 and 2010 for the Vernon Vipers of the British Columbia Hockey League.

Seniors Jeremy Langlois and Zach Davies would be crucial, as well. Langlois, a forward from Tempe, Ariz., was QU's leader in goals scored over the past two seasons, as well as a former Offensive Player of the Year for the Eastern Junior Hockey League with the New Jersey Hitmen. Davis, a defenseman, had played in 174 games over three seasons in the British Columbia Hockey League.

All of them decided to come back to Hamden. So did Pecknold, who'd received a tempting job offer of his own from the University of Massachusetts. It took an aggressive counter-offer from Quinnipiac to keep him in the fold. Although details of Pecknold's new, five-year contract with QU weren't made public, the deal is rumored to include a salary of nearly $300,000 a year.

UMass, which joined Division 1 in 1994 and appeared in its first NCAA tournament in 2007, plays in the Hockey East conference. The Minutemen had a record of 19-41-11 in the previous two seasons. UMass eventually hired John Micheletto as its head coach, for a reported base salary of $210,000.

"In the end, UMass is a premier program but I felt that Quinnipiac was the right place for me," Pecknold said. "This is my 19th year, my family is well settled here. I was in a position where I had two great opportunities and I had to pick one. I'm very happy with the one I chose."

His counterpart at Yale, Allain, had no plans to leave, either. But he would have some roster adjustments to make, just as he had for the past few years. It was the price of recruiting high-quality talent.

This year, that meant not having Brian O'Neill on the team. O'Neill had graduated and signed as a free agent with the Los Angeles Kings, taking his 163 career points with him.

"Three years ago we lost (Mark) Arcobello and (Sean) Backman; two years ago it was (Broc) Little and (Denny) Kearney," Allain said. "We have some experience losing and replacing our top forwards."

Luckily, Yale would have senior Miller leading the way. He'd led the team in assists for two years running, and he'd have plenty of guys to pass to this year.

As a sophomore, Kenny Agostino had scored a pair of huge, last-minute goals in consecutive games. Antoine Laganiere, a senior from Quebec, had tons of experience in the program; he'd played in all 34 games as a freshman, during Yale's 2011 season, and he was coming off a conference playoff series in which he'd scored five goals against Princeton.

"We're excited about the group we have," Allain said. "We have eight freshmen, three on the blue line, but our expectations are we'll be better than we were last year."

Yes—but which team from last year? The one that had struggled for a big chunk of the season or the one that finished the regular season strong?

As the season began it was a little of both. After an overtime tie and a win at the Ivy League Showcase at Brown, Yale lost badly at Dartmouth, 7-4. The very next day, the Bulldogs showed up at Boston's Bright Center to play No. 13 Harvard, and they were angry.

Yale had a blistering 49 shots in the game, winning 5-1. Miller had three assists, and the line of Miller, Agostino and junior Jesse Root was responsible for four of Yale's goals. Miller was particularly assertive in helping Yale gain an early lead. After killing a penalty that started 19 seconds into the game, the captain carried in over the blueline and cut to the high slot before feigning right and passing left to Root, who fired a shot into the top of the net.

Yale clearly wore Harvard down in the upset, scoring three times in the final period. As for its own defense, Malcolm had 28 saves and held Harvard scoreless on four power plays. These were quality moves that boded well for pressure situations later in the season.

Not that Yale's coach was ready to hand out tickets to the Frozen Four just yet. "We had a quick start, but we also had to kill three penalties in the first 12 minutes of the game," he said. "We were more aggressive up ice and protected the puck better tonight."

Then Yale went out and lost its home opener to lowly Clarkson, 1-0. In characteristic fashion, Allain called it "a step backwards."

It was something of a pattern, really. Yale would reel off four wins, including two overtime victories against nationally-ranked Denver and Colorado College, in Colorado, and then suffer a lopsided loss to Rensselaer, 6-1. One could look at it a couple of ways. Yale was struggling with consistency from game to game. But it also was proving that it could skate with anybody.

In the process, Laganiere was putting on an offensive clinic, the defense was strong and the team's mental and physical toughness was earning rewards late in games and in overtime. By the time Yale swept the regular season series with Harvard in mid-January, it was ranked No. 12.

"You come into a culture like this, it makes you want to work just as hard as everybody else," said senior forward Josh Balch. "You don't want to be the person who's letting your teammates down. You want to make sure you're helping everyone out."

But here's the thing. The team up the road was looking even better.

Quinnipiac had an aura of optimism, from the first day of practice. Perhaps that was because it had a game that day, which it won against a formidable program. QU beat Maine 2-1, on the road.

The following two games were a split at home to Robert Morris. Yet even in the loss, the Bobcats fired off 48 shots on goal.

Next up was Ohio State, a big school in a big conference with no small notoriety. Quinnipiac dominated much of the contest, but allowed Ohio State to come away with a tie on a third period chip shot over Hartzell's shoulder. Hartzell was proving to be a key in the team's penalty killing unit, which had been perfect thus far in the young season.

Pecknold noted that his squad had held its own against "a ton of talent. You're looking at seven or eight kids on that Ohio State roster that have a chance to play in the NHL one day. We did a nice job of shutting them down."

However, the team still hadn't scored on the power play. "I think we're moving the puck well and we're getting chances, which is always a good thing," Peca said. "If we weren't getting chances, it would be different. We just have to bear down and start putting the puck in the net."

Peca backed up his words the following day in a rematch with the Buckeyes. It was a game that featured two goals by Langlois, a goal by Peca and a 21-save gem by Hartzell.

"I think it could have been better with a sweep," Peca said. "I think we deserved to win last night's game. You can't win them all. We responded today really well."

That statement spoke volumes. To a man, Quinnipiac was setting its sights high. And although Peca didn't know it at the time, he and his buddies were about to test that notion of not being able to win every game.

CHAPTER EIGHT

Going in Different Directions

THE TWO REGULAR season meetings between Quinnipiac and Yale could hardly have been more one-sided.

The annual games, which lately had taken on the feel of a neighborhood grudge matches, were mini dramas all their own. They had national implications, local indignations and no small amount of personal frustrations.

Game one came on Feb. 2, at Ingalls Rink.

Quinnipiac was riding high. It hadn't lost since early November, and its attention was just as much on overtaking No. 1 ranked Minnesota as it was on the Bulldogs.

"We'll let you guys worry about the polls," Pecknold said. "For us, it's all about the Pairwise."

Smart man, as ever. As long as Quinnipiac led the Pairwise Rankings, it would get the premier position in the upcoming NCAA tournament.

Yale, on the other hand, was hurting. Just one night earlier, starting goalie Malcolm exited a game against Princeton in the first period with a leg injury. Less than three minutes into the game, in fact.

That put senior Nick Maricic in at goal. Luckily for the team, Maricic had acquitted himself well, and Yale beat Princeton 4-2. "We didn't get rattled, we stuck with the plan and eventually were able to break through in the end," Allain reflected.

Maricic, who'd only played in four games all season, also seemed well aware of his situation. "When you're backing up, at any point in time it could happen. This late in the year, you don't want to go in because you know the only way is if something bad happens," he said.

Naturally, the raucous crowd at Ingalls was psyched to take on big, bad Quinnipiac, no matter the circumstances. Things looked good for

Yale early, scoring two power-play goals on the normally stingy Hartzell. Trent Ruffolo scored with a diving rebound flick at 2:53 and Stu Wilson found the net four minutes later.

Then Quinnipiac found its offense. Mike Dalhuisen hit on a power-play goal from the top of the circle with 8:06 left in the first, followed by a wrist flick goal by Cory Hibbeler in the period's closing minutes.

Maricic's luck was fading, and Yale began to rack up penalties. Quinnipiac scored on a goal from Matthew Peca midway through the second and then Ben Arnt found the net on a rebound of a Jordan Samuels-Thomas shot.

The Bobcats kept their streak alive, winning 6-2. By the end, Maricic had been replaced in goal by Connor Wilson.

"I thought it was an even game until the middle of the third period," Allain told reporters. "That's when it started to go the other way."

A Pecknold pep-talk during a time-out might have had something to do with it.

"We said a few things," Pecknold explained. "I don't remember exactly what I said, but it was more we need to be better and we're a great hockey team; there's plenty of hockey left and we're a great team. Let's go to work."

The teams continued in opposite directions for the next couple of weeks. Quinnipiac took the top spot in the national rankings and looked unstoppable, going into the Feb. 22 rematch with Yale. Meanwhile, the Bulldogs couldn't buy a win with the entire Yale endowment as collateral.

Malcolm remained injured, and neither Yale backup seemed able to get any traction in the net. As if that weren't bad enough, Yale's offense had taken an early spring break, not getting a single 5-on-5 goal in four games, despite an average 35.5 shots on goal.

Beyond local bragging rights, Yale was seriously in danger of losing a chance at an NCAA tournament bid. Its Pairwise ranking has fallen from fifth to No. 12, and only 16 teams would get a bid come March.

"When you're in a slump, you have to simplify and make sure you stick to your game," team captain Miller said. "Seniors and juniors have to make sure the younger kids know that hopefully we'll get out of it and come away with a win as soon as we can. That's not going to happen if we change our systems and go haywire. We have to calm down and play our game."

Easier said than done, particularly when you're heading up Whitney Avenue to your local rival's building, where a sea of yellow-clad fans are waiting to see you get crushed. High Point Solutions Arena opened its doors a couple of hours before game time; a small army of students had been lined up outside.

The Bobcats proceeded to put on a defensive clinic and made short work of Yale, hitting on three goals in the first period. They won 4-1 and there was no doubt which team was in the driver's seat. The plan was to shoot early and often, while locking down on the other end with scary-good defense.

"We knew coming in that they have been shaky," Quinnipiac sophomore Matthew Peca said. "We saw that the last time we played them, and they had other games recently when they pulled a goalie and put a backup in. We knew we had to shoot the puck, and we did it pretty well."

Peca netted the first goal, followed by Kellen Jones and Travis St. Denis.

"We're in a funk right now and not playing as well as we need to play," Allain said later. "You earn results. Right now, that's why we're not getting results."

CHAPTER NINE

The Road to Atlantic City

KEVIN BUI WAS summoned to coach Rand Pecknold's office in the spring of 2009. The news, from a hockey standpoint, would be grim.

Bui had just finished his freshman season as a part-time player for Quinnipiac. The season was into its fourth month before he cracked the lineup for the first time, and he would dress for only 11 games. One of the team's hardest workers and amongst its brightest minds, he was also the last player signed in his class. And when a rules snafu forced Pecknold to trim someone from the Bobcats' roster, Bui was the choice.

"He said 'Kevin, we have to cut our roster because of Title IX and unfortunately, you're the odd man out'," Bui said. "That was a tough day. You don't want to hear you're getting released from the team that you made a commitment to."

Bui was expendable. Being told you're not quite good enough is never an easy thing to hear, especially for someone accustomed to being a star.

Playing for the Drumheller Dragons in his native Alberta, Canada, Bui was indispensible. He was named the team's most valuable player two years running, leading them in scoring in 2006-07. He won the Iron Man Award for starting 182 consecutive games. The Dragons booster club voted him winner of the Fan Favorite award.

Despite his success, the window to play Division I hockey was closing fast. Once a player hits age 21, he isn't allowed to begin a new Junior 'A' hockey season. Bui had exhausted his eligibility with no scholarship offers. He was exploring Division III opportunities in the United States when he got a call at the 11th hour.

Ben Syer, then Pecknold's top assistant, had good news. Clay Harvey, an incoming Quinnipiac recruit, was delaying his enrollment by a year to play another year of Junior hockey in British Columbia. Syer, who had scouted Bui on a couple of occasions, was offering him a roster spot. Bui accepted.

"I owe a little to Clay," Bui says. The two would become good friends and roommates in Hamden.

Pecknold felt bad dropping Bui. He offered assistance if he wanted to transfer to another hockey school. Deep down, he wanted Bui to stick around. Pecknold said he'd hold a roster spot so Bui could rejoin the team the following spring.

"In Kevin's case, he said 'Coach, I love it here. I want to stay and get better and I'll get to a point where I play more.' I said great, I hope it happens," Pecknold said. "In this case, it did happen. It's a great story."

Unable to practice with the team during his season off, he worked six days a week with Quinnipiac strength and conditioning coach Brijesh Patel. He skated on his own. On game days, he wore a suit and tie and served as a student manager, assisting in whatever way he could.

He returned to the roster for the fall of 2010, though his playing time continued to be sporadic over the next two seasons. He scored a couple of clutch goals in big games as a senior. As a fifth-year graduate student, he not only became a regular on the fourth line but emerged as one of the most clutch goal-scorers in team history.

"I'm glad I took that year off," Bui said a day before Quinnipiac left for the Frozen Four. "If I didn't, I wouldn't be here today."

Quinnipiac, as the runaway regular season champion, earned a first-round bye in the ECAC playoffs. It would wind up playing host to Cornell in a best-of-3 first-round series at High Point Solutions Arena. The Big Red swept Princeton on the road in the first round. On paper, as a ninth-seed against the No. 1 team in the country, it seemed like a mere formality.

But Cornell, loaded with size, talent and led by Mike Schafer, one of the most successful coaches in league history, was hardly a pushover. The series opener proved as much.

Brian Ferlin, a sophomore forward and draft pick of the Boston Bruins, had two of Cornell's three second-period goals while junior goalie Andy Iles was unflappable in preserving the lead as the Big Red held on for a 3-2 win.

Quinnipiac, the nation's No. 1 team, was on the brink of a humiliating early exit. And Schafer, an 18-year veteran whose teams regularly make the NCAA tournament, knew it.

"I know being in the position they're in, how much pressure there is to get to Atlantic City as a program right now," Schafer said after the game. "We can kind of play with that carefree mentality, and it's happened maybe once in my coaching career. (Quinnipiac) carries an awful lot of burden and pressure. We need to use that to our advantage in tomorrow's game."

Yet for all of Schafer's coaching savvy, he unwittingly lit a fire in the Quinnipiac locker room. The team was stunned to hear the ECAC had suspended Bryce Van Brabant, the Bobcats' bruising freshman forward, for a first-period hit on Cornell's Eric Axell. No penalty had been called on the play, but Axell was lost for the game after being hit in the head from behind.

The league decision came after a video review of the play.

Quinnipiac was irked. The players and coaches knew Schafer had sent video of the play to the league office, and he'd done so without the courtesy of even an email. To the Bobcats, it came off as underhanded and sneaky.

The tone of the series completely changed that night for Game 2. Play was physical and chippy. Words were exchanged on the ice between players and coaches. The Bobcats, already leading 2-0 after the first period, scored seven unanswered goals in the second period. Quinnipiac didn't just want to win, it wanted to prove a point. At the end of the second, a fight broke out that resulted in a combined nine game misconducts. Four more were issued in the third period. The final score, Quinnipiac 10, Cornell 0, was one of the worst beatings in ECAC playoff history.

Any images Game 2 had evoked of Reg Dunlop, Ogie Oglethorpe and the Hanson brothers were left on the ice. Both teams got back to hockey in the third and deciding game of the series; Cornell, looking to keep its season alive, Quinnipiac desperate to avoid being bounced in the quarterfinals of its own tournament and all the implications for a program battling negative national perception.

Cornell led 1-0 after the first period; 2-1 after two. As time clicked toward one minute left in regulation, Pecknold pulled Hartzell for an extra attacker. The Bobcats, dominant at even strength, got what they were looking for when Clay Harvey, working a rebound on Iles from in close, pushed the puck home to tie the score with 64 seconds remaining.

Iles made 60 saves, and single-handedly kept Cornell in the game through the first overtime period and five minutes of a second.

Quinnipiac was thoroughly in control, pumping 14 shots on Iles in the opening minutes of the second overtime before Loren Barron found Bui open with a cross-ice pass through the neutral zone.

Bui, legs still fresh, zipped past the Cornell defense for a breakaway and scored the game winner. High Point Solutions Arena, still packed despite the late hour on a Sunday night, erupted into delirium.

Bui, once dropped from the roster, cemented his legacy.

"It couldn't have happened to a better person," Pecknold said. "He can do anything."

And it was the late-third period goal by Harvey, whose delayed enrollment was directly responsible for Bui landing at Quinnipiac in the first place, once again providing a chance for him to succeed.

While Quinnipiac was surviving by the skin of its teeth, Yale advanced with little drama a few miles away at Ingalls Rink.

St. Lawrence had been wildly inconsistent in the regular season. Yale had been more consistent, at least until goaltender Jeff Malcolm went down with a knee injury the first weekend in February. The Bulldogs had lost all five games without their senior goalie. His return on Feb. 23 sparked a three-game win streak to end the regular season.

Yale, at full strength, was a bear for any opponent. Still, many around the league felt the Saints might pull the upset. With two of the nation's top three scorers in forwards Greg Carey and Kyle Flanagan, St. Lawrence was indeed dangerous.

But it proved no match for a Yale team clicking on all cylinders.

Carey and Flanagan were non-factors in the opening game. Yale played what could have been considered a perfect game, marred only by the fact that the Saints scored first.

But the Bulldogs top line of Andrew Miller, Jesse Root and Kenny Agostino would go on to combine for four goals and six assists. The Saints had no answer for senior Antoine Laganiere, who verified his status as an elite undrafted free agent by chipping in a goal and an assist while nearly outshooting St. Lawrence himself—he finished with 10 shots on goal in the game, the Saints had 13.

Yale never let up, closing out the series a night later with a 3-0 victory thanks to a goal and an assist by sophomore defenseman Tommy Fallen and a shutout by Malcolm, securing a trip to the semifinals.

Yale had enjoyed great success at the ECAC semifinals under Keith Allain. At Albany, N.Y. in 2009, the program's first trip past the quarterfinals in 11 years, it accentuated a championship with a 5-0 whitewash of Cornell. Two years later, Yale, the top-ranked team in the country, beat Colgate and Cornell by a combined 10-0.

On the heels of five straight wins, all with Malcolm back in net and healthy, the Bulldogs had positioned themselves well for the NCAA tournament. If they won the ECAC title, there was a chance they could secure a No. 1 seed when the NCAA field was announced at the end of the weekend.

Of course, two losses could potentially put Yale on the outside looking in, given the volatile nature of the Pairwise Rankings.

Quinnipiac knew its postseason fate. Although it had been 11 years since its only appearance in the tournament—it earned the automatic bid from Atlantic Hockey in 2002—Quinnipiac had secured the top overall seed for the NCAA tournament no matter what happened at the ECAC Championships.

Still, much of the chatter in the week leading up to the tournament was the fact that Yale and Quinnipiac were paired on opposite sides of the bracket and could wind up meeting in the league championship game.

Atlantic City, which made the ECAC an offer it couldn't refuse to secure the annual tournament in 2011, had been an unmitigated disaster as a host site for the league tournament. Atlantic City was 90 minutes south of Princeton, the closest league school. The drive for Clarkson and St. Lawrence by bus was closer to nine hours.

Attendance had sagged in Albany, as central a location as the league could want. In Atlantic City, it was pathetic. Boardwalk Hall can be a charming building, even exciting for big events like championship boxing. But with thousands of empty seats, it came off as dingy, small-time and flat-out depressing.

The league's three-year deal was expiring, and the ECAC would return to longtime home Lake Placid, N.Y. a year later. It couldn't happen fast enough for league administrators, coaches and fans. Thought of a potential Yale vs. Quinnipiac final might provide a bit of excitement before the league hurried out the door.

But Friday would be two of the worst games played all season by the Greater New Haven entries.

Quinnipiac was listless in a 4-0 loss to seventh-seeded Brown. Things were so bad that Hartzell, named the league's player and goaltender of the year at a banquet the night before, was given an early hook after allowing the third goal. Pecknold took him to the tunnel behind the bench, giving his star player a pep talk before sending him back to his post.

Hartzell was better, but the damage had been done.

"It's almost inexplicable how badly we played," Pecknold said after the game. "We stunk. Ultimately, it's my responsibility to get these guys ready so I'll take the blame for it . . . . It was our worst game of the year. You can't have that come at a time like this."

Things were no better for third-seeded Yale. No. 4 seed Union, another team on a hot streak, jumped out to an early lead and steamrolled the Bulldogs 5-0.

"I'm surprised," Allain said after the game. "I know we're a better hockey team than what you saw out here tonight. You have to give Union credit. There are two teams on the ice, and they made us look bad tonight. But I know our guys. We're better than what you saw and we'll be better tomorrow night."

Yale and Quinnipiac would meet. But it would be for third place, a consolation game that meant nothing to the Bobcats and almost everything for Yale. Losing to Union had put the Bulldogs in a precarious position. A contender for a No. 1 seed in the NCAAs only hours earlier, Yale still had a crack at earning a No. 2 seed with a win. But a loss to Quinnipiac may well have knocked the Bulldogs completely out the door.

Pecknold used the game to rest banged up starters Matthew Peca and Mike Dalhuisen. But he also used Hartzell. Although not sharp a day earlier, the senior goalie was back on his game against Yale. He was aided when two apparent goals by the Bulldogs were disallowed, and upheld by video review.

"We didn't want to go to the NCAAs with two straight losses," Hartzell said. "We looked at this like it was a championship game."

The 3-0 Quinnipiac win appeared devastating to Yale's postseason hopes. As league championship games played out across the country, there would be one final chance for the Bulldogs.

Michigan, on the verge of missing its first NCAA tournament in 22 years, had gone on a run for the ages in the Central Collegiate Hockey Association. Although below .500 for the season, the Wolverines' nine-game unbeaten streak put them in the CCHA final against Notre Dame. A Michigan win would give them the league's automatic NCAA berth, leaving Yale home. A Notre Dame win would save the final at-large spot for the Bulldogs.

The moments after the loss to Quinnipiac were tense around the Yale locker room. Allain didn't bother to attend the post-game press conference. Yale players showered and made a bee line to the bus.

League administrators were upset. Ed Krajewski, the ECAC's assistant commissioner, kept a room full of media waiting before sheepishly announcing that Yale, in fact, would not be answering questions.

If the Bulldogs felt helpless during their four-hour bus ride back to New Haven Saturday night, it's because they were. Yale's fate was in the hands of Notre Dame.

On Sunday afternoon, several Yale players met at the local Buffalo Wild Wings to watch the CCHA final. Some kept their distance, the vulnerability of the situation too much to swallow. Allain kept tabs on the score via his lap top.

When Notre Dame closed out its 3-1 victory, Yale was back from the dead. It became official a few hours later when the announcement of the bracket and matchups was broadcast.

Quinnipiac attended the tournament selection show's live taping at ESPN's headquarters in Bristol, a few miles north of Hamden. Yale, as it did in years past when it qualified, had a private viewing.

None of the broadcasters gave either team any chance of winning. Dave Starman, an in-studio analyst for the network's NCAA tournament coverage, said UMass Lowell was his choice to win the championship. Barry Melrose, a former NHL coach and analyst with a reputation for glossing over his college duties, began his breakdown of Quinnipiac by referring to its star goalie as "Hartnell." His choice to win it all was Wisconsin.

Their respective struggles in the ECAC tournament had annulled what little respect Yale and Quinnipiac had accumulated with their tremendous seasons to that point.

National opinion would soon change.

CHAPTER TEN

The Tournament

BEN SMITH SETTLED into a seat at Conte Forum in Chestnut Hill, Mass. in January. Yale was about to play at Boston College, the defending national champion looking to win its fourth crown in six seasons. Smith, the four-time U.S. Olympic hockey coach was there on a scouting assignment.

The game would end in a 3-3 tie. But there was no doubt which team had the clear edge in play, scoring chances and flat-out talent. And it sure as rain wasn't Boston College. Yale finished with 48 shots on goal, creating at will against the Eagles, while allowing only 22.

A night later Smith was on another scouting assignment at Boston University, where he sat next to longtime Terriers' radio broadcaster Bernie Corbett in the press box.

"He said 'Bernie, I think I just saw the best team in the country last night,'" Corbett said. "He said, 'The road to the national championship just might run through New Haven.'"

Smith may have been convinced Yale was the nation's best team. It was hardly a popular opinion heading into the NCAA West Regional.

If Yale's poor showing in Atlantic City wasn't enough, the draw at Van Andel Arena in Grand Rapids, Mich. was particularly harsh. The Bulldogs, seeded 15th of 16 teams in the field, had to play second overall seed Minnesota, a five-time national champion, in the opening game. And if they got past the loaded Gophers, it would likely be North Dakota, a seven-time national champion, in the regional final.

As it practiced at Ingalls Rink that week, Yale was supremely confident. Sure, Minnesota was fast and it was talented. It also played right into the Bulldogs' wheelhouse. Yale could skate with anyone.

History had proven that. There was the Boston College game, as well as a pair of overtime wins in November at Denver and Colorado College.

In fact, Allain's teams seemed to have the powerful Western Collegiate Hockey Association's number over the years, losing only one of the previous eight games. That included a stunning 3-2 victory over North Dakota at the NCAA Northeast Regional in Worcester, Mass. in 2010.

Yale's strategy was to be the aggressor, dictate the pace and pressure the Gophers into turnovers.

"If we show up, and everyone is going like they can, it could be a good opportunity to surprise some people," said Yale sophomore defenseman Tommy Fallen.

There were already a few storylines brewing as Yale headed to the airport for its flight. Captain Andrew Miller, forward Clint Bourbonais and defenseman Ryan Obuchowski were returning to their home state of Michigan for the first time as collegians. Fallen, the lone Minnesota native for Yale, had played with or against most of the current Gopher roster.

Things were about to get really interesting.

Kenny Agostino, a junior and member of Yale's top skating line with Miller and Jesse Root, was in the midst of his finest season. His point production had increased, not always easy for someone who came in at a point-per game as a sophomore. He was strong on the puck, his game physical. The scouts noticed.

He went to bed at the team hotel in Grand Rapids as property of the Pittsburgh Penguins, the team that drafted him in the fifth round a few months before his arrival at Yale three years earlier. He awoke to find his NHL rights had been traded in the wee hours of the morning to Calgary, along with St. Cloud State's Ben Hanowski, for NHL icon Jarome Iginla.

A few questions about the trade were raised after Yale's practice session at Van Andel Arena. Agostino did his best to put it to the back burner and focus on the next day's game.

"It's a pretty cool thing to be a part of," Agostino said. "The guys were good about it that morning, at breakfast, when it happened. I realized at that time it was important to put it in the back of my mind and just worry about playing Minnesota."

On Friday afternoon, after a scoreless first period, Agostino struck first against Minnesota. His even-strength goal just more than seven minutes into the second gave Yale the lead. Eight minutes later, on a power play, defenseman Gus Young made it a two-goal game.

The Gophers, unwilling to roll over and go quietly, put together a furious third-period rally to send the game to overtime. Nate Schmidt's power-play goal came at 8:12, five minutes before Zach Budish evened the score.

Minnesota seemed to have the momentum heading into the extra session. Yale never gave it a chance. The Gophers won the opening faceoff in overtime, but Agostino aggressively chased the puck deep into the Minnesota zone. He stole the puck behind the goal and quickly sent a pass through the crease. Jesse Root banged it into the net for a 3-2 win.

Many Minnesota players hadn't even situated themselves on the bench. Coach Don Lucia said he never even saw the winning play. It was the fastest overtime goal in NCAA tournament history. In a mere nine seconds, Yale, practically an after-thought in the field, captured the nation's attention.

Halfway across the country in Providence, site of the East Regional, Boston College had just finished its practice day interviews. Players exited the dais into the media work room, pausing to catch a glimpse of the overtime. The Eagles were surprised at the quickness of Root's goal, but not that Yale had beaten Minnesota.

"For so long, New England hockey in general has been pretty much BC and BU," said Boston College captain Pat Mullane, who grew up a short drive from both Yale and Quinnipiac. "I think it's great for Connecticut hockey."

Yale would face North Dakota in the West Regional final on Saturday, the puck drop just before the start of Quinnipiac's opening game against Canisius at the East Regional.

The Fighting Sioux needed a third-period rally to get past Niagara in the opener, and had no reason to take Yale lightly. Dave Hakstol, in his ninth season as North Dakota coach, had a front-row seat to the Bulldogs 3-2 stunner in Worcester three years earlier. Goaltending had been the Bulldogs Achilles heel that winter, but little used Ryan Rondeau stoned the Fighting Sioux while Denny Kearney had a pair of goals. Andrew Miller, Antoine Laganiere, Josh Balch and Colin Dueck, then freshmen, all played in that game.

North Dakota took an early lead on Corban Knight's first-period goal, which stood as the game's lone tally into the third period. Yale had been dictating the pace. It was only a matter of time before it broke through.

Balch tied it with 7:35 remaining. Unchecked by the Sioux while in front of the net, he cleaned up a puck sent by teammate Anthony Day from the halfboards that bounded off the goaltender's pads and onto Balch's stick.

A power play two minutes later led to Root's go-ahead goal, set up by Andrew Miller carrying the puck through the North Dakota zone. Root steered it through the slot toward the outside, turned and fired a shot home to give Yale the lead.

Day and Stu Wilson, on a 2-on-1 break, padded the lead. Day took the shot, which took a high bounce off the goalie's pads and was knocked in by Wilson. Agostino's empty-net goal made it 4-1, clinching Yale's first trip to the Frozen Four since the days of coach Murray Murdoch 61 years earlier.

While Yale was celebrating, Quinnipiac was sweating. Canisius, a middle-of-the-pack team in lightly-regarded Atlantic Hockey, had gotten hot at the right time. The Golden Griffins season record was 11-18-5 entering the final weekend of the regular season, and the team simply wanted a sweep to ensure home ice for the first round of league playoffs.

By the time they arrived in Providence as league champions, Canisius was a trendy upset pick. Quinnipiac's status atop the polls and Pairwise didn't stop many experts from picking it to lose its first game.

"A lot of people, myself included, think (Quinnipiac) might be the worst No. 1 seed in NCAA history," wrote Ryan Lambert of Yahoo! Sports.

The pressure seemed to get the best of Quinnipiac. Despite taking an early lead, Canisius beat goalie Eric Hartzell for two quick-strike goals early in the second to take a 2-1 lead into the third. When Kyle Gibbons scored an unassisted goal early in the third period, it appeared the experts might have been right about the Bobcats.

But with plenty of time left, Quinnipiac refused to panic.

"Everyone's sort of looking at each other," said forward Jordan Samuels-Thomas. "We worked so hard, blessed with such an opportunity. No one wanted to go out this way."

Matthew Peca single-handedly swung the momentum in Quinnipiac's favor. Moving on net after a pass from Connor Jones, he kept the puck on his forehand and chipped it over the shoulder of goalie Tony Capobianco at an ungodly angle to bring the Bobcats within 3-2.

Samuels-Thomas tied it with a wrist shot a little over 2 minutes later. The game-winner came from (who else?) Kevin Bui, cleaning up a rebound from Bryce Van Brabant with 5:32 remaining, giving Quinnipiac a 4-3 lead and sending it on to the regional final.

The prevailing feeling was more relief than satisfaction. Quinnipiac knew it had to be better against Union with a spot in the Frozen Four at stake.

"We're happy we won the game," said Hartzell. "But I would say we played a 'C-plus' game. Defense wins championships and we have to limit our turnovers. There are going to be turnovers, but they have to be smaller goal-scoring opportunities than we let up tonight. Every time we had a turnover, they had a serious opportunity to score. The boys know that, they'll be fired up to fix that and play great (today)."

Union presented another challenge. It had made its own historic trip to the Frozen Four in Tampa, Fla. a year earlier, and got its act together at the right time by punishing Yale and Brown to win the ECAC championship in Atlantic City.

Boston College, in search of its third national title in four years, was no match at the East Regional, barely putting up a fight in a 5-1 loss. The Dutchmen, losers to Ferris State in the national semifinals a year earlier, had aspirations to get back and make amends in Pittsburgh.

Peca left nothing to chance, putting Union away almost immediately. His natural hat trick, over a span of 3:12 midway through the first, was the fastest in NCAA history. It was a 5-0 game after two periods, and a 5-1 final.

Quinnipiac, which had never won an NCAA game prior to the season, was joining backyard rival Yale at the Frozen Four. Even more interesting was that the two Greater New Haven schools matched up on opposite sides of the bracket, meaning if both took care of business in the semifinals, they could meet for the national championship.

CHAPTER ELEVEN

Party in Pittsburgh

ANDREW MILLER HAS always had options. Whether selecting his future path or waiting out the defense to perfectly distribute a puck, his diligence and patience consistently brings about the intended result.

As a student at Cranbrook Kingswood School in the Detroit suburb of Bloomfield Hills, Miller was the best high school hockey player in Michigan. He was also the best lacrosse player.

Major college opportunities came in both sports. Miller identified hockey as a greater return on his investment. He dropped lacrosse.

Established hockey powers Colorado College and Miami-Ohio showed interest in Miller, who would be named Michigan's "Mr. Hockey" after 37 goals, 45 assists and a state championship as a senior. Yale was his at the top of his list. While able to draw on the experience of Andy Weidenbach, an All-ECAC forward at Yale and Cranbrook's hockey coach, he also understood the value of a Yale degree.

Miller put off enrollment to hone his game in the Junior 'A' United States Hockey League. He scored 41 points his first year with the Chicago Steel, coached by ex-NHL player Steve Poabst. His point total doubled the next season and he was named USA Hockey's national junior player of the year.

"It helped an extravagant amount," Miller said of his time in the USHL. "My coach was a great guy who understood how to develop players and I got every opportunity to succeed."

Those opportunities would continue at Yale. Keith Allain noticed immediately that Miller viewed the game differently than the average player. His passing was not only precise, but prescient. Miller had an ability to see two and three plays ahead.

He scored a goal is his first game; added three assists a week later. Four games into his Yale career, he was centering one of the top-scoring lines in the game.

"He has a chance to be as good as anyone in college hockey," Allain said at the time.

By the time he was a senior, Miller had been an essential figure in two of Yale's best teams.

The Bulldogs stunned North Dakota at the NCAA Northeast Regional in 2010 to earn a date with Boston College and a berth in the Frozen Four on the line. Miller, as a freshman, had four assists in a wild 9-7 loss.

A year later Yale came up just shy of college hockey's Promised Land again. As the top seed in the East Regional in Bridgeport, the Bulldogs beat Air Force in overtime to make the regional final again. But a 5-3 loss to Minnesota-Duluth prevented Yale's 27-win team from the Frozen Four.

As a junior, Miller played on the only mediocre Yale team in a five-year span. Yale's senior class cherished its final shot. A burning desire to make up for the missed opportunities of the past ate away at forwards Antoine Laganiere and Josh Balch, defenseman Colin Dueck and goalie Jeff Malcolm.

In Miller they had a perfect captain; a leader who'd earned and commanded full respect of teammates. At the Frozen Four, to be played at Pittsburgh's Consol Energy Center, Miller would cement his legacy and stake a claim as perhaps the greatest player in Yale hockey history.

Yale and Quinnipiac would be matched up on opposite sides of the Frozen Four bracket. If both took care of business in the semifinals, Yale against UMass Lowell; Quinnipiac against St. Cloud State, the national title game would double as Connecticut's state championship.

Yale was loose and confident in the hours before it took the ice. It was a battle-tested group accustomed to big games.

UMass Lowell had experience, too. A three-time NCAA Division II champion, the River Hawks had upgraded to Division I in 1983. Life in Hockey East, alongside well-oiled machines Boston University, Boston College, Maine and New Hampshire, proved tough sledding for nearly 30 years.

But in 2012, UMass Lowell made the NCAA tournament for the first time in 16 years. It stunned top-seeded Miami-Ohio at the East

Regional in Bridgeport, losing to Union in the national quarterfinals a night later.

The 2012-13 season was historic. UMass Lowell won its first Hockey East regular season title, capping it with a win over Boston University for the tournament championship. A suffocating defensive unit, the River Hawks hammered Wisconsin by a five-goal margin in its NCAA opener and shutout New Hampshire to reach the Frozen Four.

When the Las Vegas Hotel and Casino released its betting lines prior to the Frozen Four, UMass Lowell was the odds-on favorite to win it all at 8-to-5. Yale was the longshot at 5-to-1.

But as the game progressed, Yale showed why Vegas has no business posting college hockey lines. It was all Yale. But a scary moment, followed by 14-second lapse, both in the second period, kept the Eli faithful on the edge of their seats.

Yale led 2-0 after one period thanks to goals by freshman Mitch Witek and senior Antoine Laganiere. UMass Lowell star Riley Wetmore stole a puck in the second and went on a breakaway. He didn't score, but had Yale holding its breath when he crashed into the legs of goalie Jeff Malcolm on the play.

Two months earlier, Malcolm suffered a knee injury when an out-of-control Princeton player crashed into him on an almost identical play. Malcolm missed the next five games. Yale lost all of them, proving their starting goaltender was indispensible to the team's success.

Malcolm wasn't injured on this play. But 10 minutes later, he allowed two quick-strike goals that got UMass Lowell back in the game. After two periods, the score was tied at 2-2. As the third period played out, it became apparent that barring an all-out meltdown, the winning Yale goal was imminent.

"There was never any unease or sense of doubt," Kenny Agostino said.

Yale pumped 16 shots on goal in the third period; the River Hawks mustered only three. Only Connor Hellebuyck, the brilliant freshman goaltender, kept his team in the game. He'd overcome early jitters and not allowed a puck in his net since the final minute of the first period.

Yale knew he couldn't do it all himself forever. Just under 7 minutes into overtime, with Yale on a 7-0 shot advantage, the captain delivered.

Yale freshman forward Carson Cooper sent a puck off the boards into the neutral zone. Miller tracked it down and chipped it around a UMass Lowell defender, cutting back toward center ice for a breakaway. As he zipped across the goalmouth, he slipped the puck through the legs of Hellebuyck for the game-winning goal.

Earlier in the game Miller broke the school record for career assists when he helped set up Witek's goal. Now, he had the biggest goal in program history. Yale, the birthplace of intercollegiate hockey 117 years earlier, would play for its first national championship.

"It was the right scenario," Yale senior forward Josh Balch said. "He's a great leader; a great player. If there was any player I wanted to do it for us, I'm happy it was him."

Sounds of celebration reverberated inside Quinnipiac's locker room at the Consol Energy Center. The Bobcats soon learned Yale had advanced. Goaltender Eric Hartzell was excited, and knew his teammates were thinking the same thing: take care of business, and it's a game against Yale for the national title.

St. Cloud State was an intriguing matchup. As regular-season champion of the Western Collegiate Hockey Association, a conference typically dominated by Minnesota, North Dakota, Wisconsin and Denver, the Huskies were dangerous.

St. Cloud State also had Drew LeBlanc, a senior forward who would win the Hobey Baker Award a day later as the nation's outstanding player, beating out Boston College forward Johnny Gaudreau and Hartzell.

Pecknold, in his pregame locker room speech, was confident and calm. His wife, Nikki, had given birth to the couple's fourth child, Rex Thomas Pecknold, in the down time between the East Regional and the Frozen Four. Playing for a spot in the national championship game was only the second most exciting thing to happen in his week. The Bobcats, following their coach's lead, took the ice with the firm belief they were the better team. Like it did against Union in the East Regional final, Quinnipiac made quick work of the opponent.

Jordan Samuels-Thomas had languished for two seasons at Bowling Green and another as a practice player in Hamden. As a transfer student, he was ineligible for the 2011-12 season. His impact at Quinnipiac would be felt immediately, scoring the game-winning goal against Maine in his first game.

Crucial goals would become his calling card.

The game wasn't two minutes old when Samuels-Thomas controlled a loose puck behind the St. Cloud net, swooped around and jammed it past the goaltender to open the scoring.

Minutes later, Samuels-Thomas went for another wrap-around. This time, the puck kicked out to senior Ben Arnt in the high slot for another goal.

And it wasn't long before Quinnipiac added another goal, Jeremy Langlois cleaning up a rebound left by Zach Davies.

Just 11 minutes, 19 seconds into the game, Quinnipiac led 3-0. The remainder was a mere formality. St. Cloud State's lone attempt to get back in it, a goal by Joey Benik in the second period, was fleeting. Kellen Jones recaptured the three-goal lead before the period was finished.

A 4-1 Quinnipiac victory meant it would be an all-Connecticut national championship matchup.

The rest of the nation, many so unwilling to accept either as a threat just two weeks earlier, would be watching the live TV broadcast.

CHAPTER TWELVE

Game Day

THE AFTERNOON OF the national championship game was quite a sight. At the downtown Pittsburgh Marriott, hundreds of Yale parents and alumni gathered in the lobby for pregame drinks and food.

Across the street at the Consol Energy Center, they rolled out the red carpet. Fans gathered outside ropes and stanchions to watch players walk the few steps from the bus to the arena entrance. Pep bands blasted their fight song; cheerleaders waved pom-poms; the giant Bulldog and Bobcat mascots worked the crowd.

Fan support for Yale and Quinnipiac is often contrasting.

Quinnipiac has local community support, but is driven by an enthusiastic and vocal student section.

Yale gets some support from its student body, but the bulk of its fan base is older alumni, townies and youth hockey families. The school hadn't even planned on subsidizing the cost of transportation for students to get to Pittsburgh, leaving many wondering if Quinnipiac's student section would again dwarf that of Yale. Only a last minute decision by the Yale administration to coordinate busses allowed students an affordable option to get to the Frozen Four.

"The full busses to Pittsburgh and packed viewing party at Payne Whitney suggest that Yale students care more about athletics than our administration assumes," read an op-ed column in the Yale Daily News. "Yale should view the excitement and college unity generated by this momentous weekend as a glimpse of what sports really means to this campus."

Yale's student body and alumni were all in on this one. Same at Quinnipiac. On occasion, as happens when bitter rivals get together, tension boils over. During the red-carpet ceremony, a Quinnipiac student and an older Yale fan got into a heated argument. They were separated before it got really ugly.

As game-time neared, the seats slowly began to fill. Every ticket had been sold. Still, some wondered if all would show up to see a national championship game between two New Haven County rivals. Those questions ended quickly. The arena was filled to its capacity of 18,184. Quinnipiac fans dressed in gold filled two large swaths of seats, directly across from a sea of Yale fans in blue.

Large crowds and an intense atmosphere is nothing new for this rivalry.

Since its inception in 2006-07, securing seats to regular season games between Yale and Quinnipiac in either New Haven or Hamden has been akin to scoring tickets to U2 or Pearl Jam. But three weeks earlier, at Boardwalk Hall in Atlantic City, the teams played in front of mostly empty seats in the ECAC Hockey consolation game.

The expansive Consol Energy Center was filled, from bottom to far-reaching upper deck. This was new territory. Matthew Peca, the dynamic sophomore forward for Quinnipiac, said the biggest crowds he'd ever played in front of were those at High Point Solutions Arena this season.

The inflated swarms of the Frozen Four had little to no effect on the players in the semifinals two nights earlier, when Yale and Quinnipiac scored convincing wins.

On the night of the finals, players from both teams went through traditional pre-game rituals and routines. Eric Hartzell juggled tennis balls off a concrete wall. A group of Quinnipiac players circled up to kick a soccer ball. Yale senior Josh Balch searched for open space in the endless hallways beneath the Consol Center to get in his stretching and wind sprints.

Yale goaltender Jeff Malcolm, so engrossed in what lie ahead, forgot his own birthday.

"I woke up this morning and didn't even realize it until one of my teammates said happy birthday," Malcolm said. "I guess I was focused."

Indeed. Malcolm would play the finest game of his life. He'd missed the two regular season games with Quinnipiac with a knee injury, and the Bobcats had beaten up on Yale backups. It became apparent early on that Malcolm was on top of his game.

The pace was fast and skilled from the get-go; exciting television for the rest of the nation watching from their homes.

Malcolm stoned Connor Jones on a Quinnipiac power play midway through the first period. Later, when a rebound kicked into the air, Malcolm batted it away with his blocker. Jeremy Langlois had a snap shot turned away, and Yale cleared the rebound away from two Bobcats in position to score. In the closing seconds of the first, Langlois breezed around a defender for a clear look at Malcolm, only to be denied again.

Early in the second, gifted scorer Matthew Peca raced toward the goal and dragged the puck around a Yale defender for an open shot. Malcolm never flinched and made the save.

When the Yale student section serenaded Malcolm with a chorus of "Happy Birthday," he responded with another big play. His pad save from point-blank range kept a Jordan Samuels-Thomas shot out of net.

"Jeff played great all night," Yale senior defenseman Colin Dueck said. "You could tell right from the start, he was feeling it. He was getting shots and he was seeing them and moving well. He made a pretty good breakaway stop (on Peca) and I knew at that point he was just closing the door."

As the game ticked past its midway point, each team got a golden chance to break the scoreless tie.

Quinnipiac had 63 seconds of a 5-on-3 that was killed off by Yale; the Bulldogs almost immediately found themselves with 73 seconds of a two-man advantage, but were unable to score.

It appeared the game would head to the third period without a goal, something that last happened in a championship game in 1968. Junior Clint Bourbonais ensured that streak would continue. He planted himself in front of the net with 3.5 seconds remaining on the clock. Defenseman Gus Young hastily sent the puck in his direction. Bourbonais extended his stick and redirected it through the legs of Hartzell.

Yale 1, Quinnipiac 0.

Bourbonais, the son of a biochemist and studying to become a biomedical engineer, sensed the tide shift.

"It's always bad for a team to give up a goal in the first or last minute of a period," he said. "That was huge. It gave us all the momentum."

A game that was shaping up as a goaltending duel between Hartzell and Malcolm had changed in an instant. Yale took the upper hand into the second intermission; Quinnipiac couldn't afford another mistake.

"It was a huge swing," Allain said. "It changed our mindset going into the third period because we had the lead and I think it changed their mindset going into the third because now they had to fight from behind."

Another unlikely hero scored the next Yale goal. Early in the third period, freshman Charles Orzetti, who had only one goal all season, fired a puck at Hartzell. The rebound kicked to the side. Orzetti chased it down. He snapped a second shot that quite literally went through Hartzell's leg pads.

"It couldn't have hit my pad any harder," Hartzell said. "I have no idea how it went in. It went right through the middle of my pad."

Over 400 miles away in New Haven, Yale fans, who filled several local establishments, knew the end was near. At a packed viewing party at Yale's Payne Whitney gymnasium, Orzetti's goal send the horde of students, alumni and faculty into delirium.

Andrew Miller, the player coach Keith Allain called the greatest playmaker he'd coached during his time at Yale, delivered the death blow. Skating through the heart of the neutral zone, Miller caught a perfect feed from linemate Kenny Agostino. Nothing stood between Miller and Hartzell.

A week earlier in Hamden, Hartzell had been asked if he knew anyone on Yale personally. He mentioned a brief on-ice interaction with Miller.

"The only acquaintance I sort of have is over the last three years I seem to have a glove save against Miller," Hartzell said. "So every time we shake hands at the end of the game, fortunately for us it's (three wins this year), he just gave me that eye and said good game and that he hated me."

There would be no glove save this time. Miller fired a wrist shot past Hartzell to make it 3-0.

Desperate to get back in the game and with time running out, Quinnipiac coach Rand Pecknold, during a 4-on-4 pulled Hartzell in favor of an extra skater. Jesse Root, a Pittsburgh kid playing the biggest game of his life right in his own backyard, scored on the empty net to make it 4-0.

Yale's student section was beside itself, leaping up and down almost in unison for what seemed like an eternity. Sensing victory, they rubbed it in by chanting "Overrated" at the silent Quinnipiac student section. When the clock expired, players mobbed Malcolm while Allain and his assistant coaches embraced each other in an extended group hug.

In 1896, Yale played the first intercollegiate hockey game against Johns Hopkins. For 117 years, that stood as the only real national milestone for the country's most ancient program. On this night, Yale reentered college hockey history.

It was the national champion.

CHAPTER THIRTEEN

The Aftermath

THE DAYS AFTER the national championship game offered little time to unwind. There were celebrations to attend and NHL offers to consider.

The Consol Energy Center apparently left quite an impression on goalie Eric Hartzell. On Sunday, less than 24 hours after the game, he signed an NHL contract with the Penguins. Days later he would become the first Quinnipiac player to suit up for an NHL game.

Yale formally greeted its fans on Monday, over 1,000 attending a championship ceremony at Ingalls Rink. Conspicuously absent from the day's festivities was Kenny Agostino. The junior forward, his NHL rights traded by the Penguins to Calgary for superstar Jarome Iginla two weeks earlier, had returned to his New Jersey home to discuss his future with family.

On Tuesday, Agostino decided to put off pro hockey another year, informing Allain he would finish his education and return to Yale. That same day, teammate Antoine Laganiere, one of the most sought-after college free agents available, agreed to a deal with Anaheim, a team whose scouting department is led by one-time Yale captain Dave Baseggio.

A day later Andrew Miller, most outstanding player at the Frozen Four, agreed to terms with the Edmonton Oilers.

In late May, Red Gendron, Yale's top assistant coach, was named head coach at Maine. Quinnipiac senior defenseman Mike Dalhuisen signed a minor-league contract with the New York Islanders, a deal which will keep him in Connecticut the following season as a member of the club's American Hockey League affiliate in Bridgeport.

Quinnipiac got good news from junior twins Kellen and Connor Jones and sophomore Matthew Peca, all of whom informed Rand Pecknold they would put off pro hockey to return to school in the fall.

Yale accepted an offer from the Boston Red Sox to throw out the first pitch at Fenway Park before that Saturday's game with Kansas City, one week after the national title game. The invitation was put on hold. The Boston Marathon bombing suspects would be captured that Friday. The Red Sox decided to hold a ceremony for the tragedy's victims and heroes prior to Saturday's game.

One of Keith Allain's first orders of business upon returning home from Pittsburgh was to express gratitude to Tim Taylor, his gravely ill friend, former coach and mentor.

During a live ESPN interview in the moments after beating Quinnipiac, Allain got a chance to thank Taylor. And in the locker room before his extensive postgame media duties, Allain called Taylor's cell phone.

"He didn't answer, but I left him a nice message," Allain said.

But Allain had something more than a TV shout-out and voice mail message.

Taylor had been diagnosed with cancer. He managed to stay intimately involved at the game's highest level through treatment, remission and eventual relapse. Three months earlier, he flew to Ufa, Russia for the World Junior Championships, the most prestigious hockey tournament for the world's best players under age 20. Taylor was USA Hockey's director of player personnel. Though very ill, he watched with delight as the team he helped construct captured gold.

By April, Taylor had been admitted to Connecticut Hospice in Branford. His relationship with Yale was irrevocably damaged in 2006. Yale administration wanted him to retire immediately after a string of losing seasons. Taylor, then 64 and with three decades of tenure at Yale, was open to retirement, but wanted one more season. He resigned under pressure.

Taylor had coached longer and won more games than any other coach in the century-old program. Humiliated, the proud and private man disassociated himself from the school.

Still, he remained close with Allain and kept close tabs on Yale hockey.

Allain, as Yale's freshman goaltender, helped secure Taylor's first career coaching victory in 1976. When Allain's playing days ended, Taylor not only persuaded him to get into coaching, but offered him a job as his assistant at Yale.

"I didn't really know what I wanted to do, and Tim called me up and said, 'I think you should come back and coach,'" Allain said. "The boost of confidence that gave me, I'm thinking, 'Geez, if Tim Taylor thinks I can coach, maybe I can coach.'"

Allain moved on from Yale to become an NHL assistant and, like Taylor, got heavily involved with USA Hockey. In 2001, he was named head coach for the U.S. National Junior Team. He asked Taylor to be his assistant. When Taylor was forced out at Yale, Allain consulted with his mentor before interviewing.

The relationship between the two was on solid ground. Taylor was able to follow the NCAA tournament action from hospice, enjoying the moment with family.

Shortly after Andrew Miller's overtime goal against UMass-Lowell in the semifinal sent Yale to the national championship game, Taylor's wife, Diana Cooke, sent an email to Allain in Pittsburgh.

"I remember the quote," Allain said. "She said Tim was 'over-the-moon' happy with our team and what we were doing.'"

The day after returning from Pittsburgh, Allain and assistant coaches Red Gendron and Dan Muse drove to visit Taylor in hospice. They brought along the NCAA championship trophy. Taylor held the trophy, even posed for pictures.

Allain's father had died in Worcester, Mass. after the first weekend of the season in late October. His father-in-law in Sweden passed just days before the start of the Frozen Four.

Allain soaked up every moment of that final visit with Taylor.

"It was a great thrill to see him with the trophy," Allain said. "It meant a lot to all of us."

Taylor passed away less than two weeks later at age 71. The Yale hockey family mourned. But the realization that Taylor had seen and enjoyed the national championship was comforting to a generation of former Bulldogs.

Quinnipiac's arrival on the national stage won't be a one-year phenomenon. The university continues to invest in the program. Among the upgrades is an NHL-caliber scoreboard with the latest HD video technology, set to be installed in time for the start of the 2013-14 season.

Holes in the lineup, most notably the one left by Hartzell, will be filled by another strong recruiting class. The line of Matthew Peca and Kellen and Connor Jones give the Bobcats one of the best trio of playmakers in the country. Quinnipiac enters the fall of 2013 with a real shot at returning to the Frozen Four in Philadelphia.

For years, a wooden sign that read "Think Lake Placid" appeared above the locker room door at Ingalls Rink. The season ambition for Yale was shooting for the ECAC semifinals, held at the same site as the 1980 "Miracle on Ice."

Appearances in the NCAA tournament were once-in-a-generation events at Yale. Not anymore. The program under Allain, with four appearances in five years, was already a regular in the field of 16. The national title was culmination of the program's revival.

Quinnipiac and Yale, both barely relevant on the national stage for years, still had legions of doubters in the fall of 2012. That all changed in one magical season.

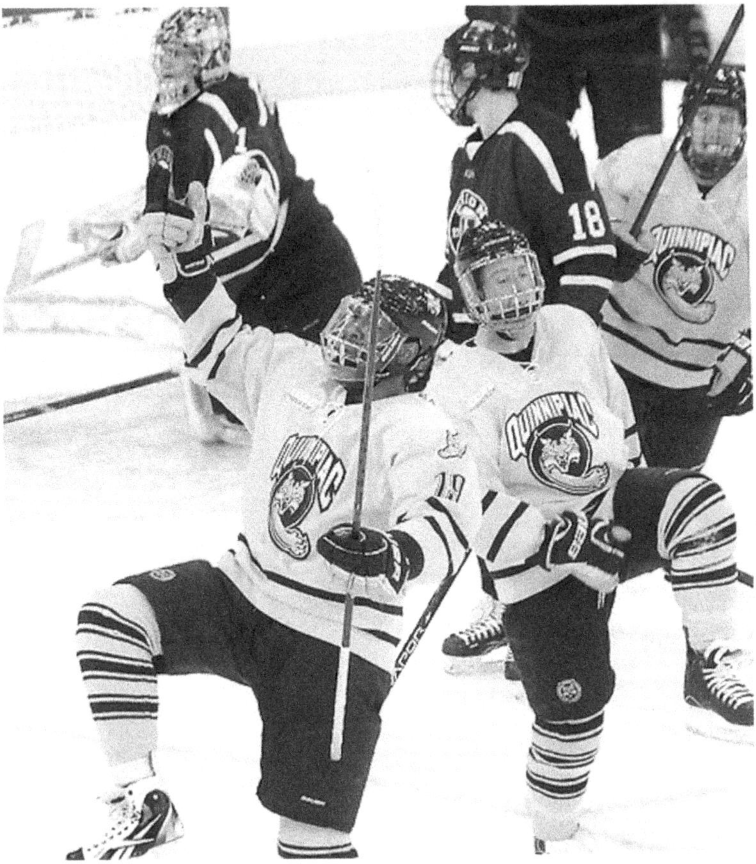

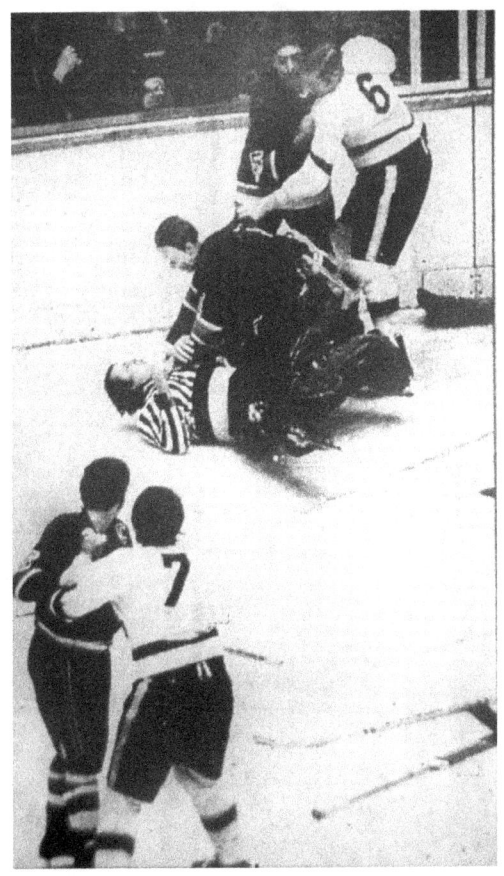

YALE NCAA & NATIONAL CHAMPIONSHIP HISTORY

- According to the NCAA Record Book, Yale has won 26 NCAA team national titles – 21 in men's golf, four in men's swimming and one in men's ice hockey.
- Yale has more NCAA team titles than any other Ivy School and the 26 are the 10th most among all Division I schools. Southern California is the Division I leader with 82 NCAA team titles.
- Prior to the 2013 men's ice hockey title, Yale's last NCAA team title came in men's swimming in 1953 under the direction of legendary head coach Robert Kiphuth.
- Yale's 21 men's golf titles are tied for the fourth most of any school in one sport. Oklahoma State leads the way with 34 wrestling team titles. The Bulldogs last won the NCAA team title in 1943.
- Yale's last NCAA title of any kind came in women's rowing in 2010 when the varsity eight won the grand final. Two members of that crew – Taylor Ritzel (USA) and Tess Gerrand (Australia) went on to compete in the 2012 Olympics in London. Ritzel won a gold medal with the U.S. eight. Yale has finished in the top-10 in the team title at the NCAA Women's Rowing Championship in 10 of the last 11 years. The Bulldogs' best team finish was second in 2004.
- Yale has won a number of national championships in non NCAA sponsored sports. In 2011, the Bulldogs won national championships in women's squash (Howe Cup) and lightweight crew (IRA).
- The Yale football team is credited with 27 national championships. The most recent came in 1927 and was awarded by the College Football Researches Association.

YALE'S NATIONAL CHAMPIONSHIP TEAMS

(all NCAA titles unless noted)

Hockey, Men
2013

Basketball, Men (2, HAF)
1901
1903

Fencing, Women (3, NIWFA)
1981-82
1983-84
1984-85

Football (27)
YEAR	Awarded by:
1872	PD
1874	NCF PD
1876	BR NCF PD
1877	NCF PD
1879	PD
1880	BR NCF PD
1881	NCF PD
1882	BR NCF PD
1883	BR HAF NCF PD
1884	HAF NCF PD
1886	HAF NCF PD
1887	BR HAF HS NCF PD
1888	BR HAF HS NCF PD
1891	BR HAF HS NCF PD
1892	BR HAF HS NCF PD

1893	PD
1894	BR HAF NCF PD
1895	PD
1897	PD
1900	BR HAF HS NCF PD
1901	PD
1902	PD
1905	CW PD
1906	BR CW PD
1907	BR CW HAF HS NCF PD
1909	BR HAF HS NCF PD
1927	CFRA

Golf, Men (21)
1897	
1898	(fall)
1902	(fall)
1905	
1906	
1907	
1908	
1909	
1910	
1911	
1912	
1913	
1915	
1924	
1925	
1926	
1931	
1932	
1933	
1936	
1943	

Heavyweight Crew (6)
1873 (V6, RAAC)
1873 (Freshman V6, RAAC)

1888 (V8, RAAC)
1897 (Freshman V8, IRA)
1977 (Varsity Pairs, IRA)
1982 (V8)

Lightweight Crew (6, all V8—The 1922 Trophy)
1987
1990
2000
2002
2005
2011

Women's Crew (11)
1979 (V8)
1981 (Novice)
1986 (Novice)
1987 (Novice)
1988 (Novice)
1988 (JV)
1993 (V4)
2007 (V8)
2008 (V8)
2009 (2V8)
2010 (V8)

Sailing, Men/Women (12, ICSA)
1947 (Dinghy)
1949 (Dinghy)
1950 (Dinghy)
1949 (Dinghy)
1950 (Dinghy)
1975 (Dinghy)
2004 (women's)
2005 (women's single handed)
2008 (men's single handed)
2009 (women's)
2010 (women's single handed)
2011 (men's single handed)
Note: became varsity sport in 2002

Squash, Men (7, CSA)
1946
1950
1952
1958
1961
1989
1990

Squash, Women (7, CSA)
1977
1986
1992
2004
2005
2006
2011

Swimming, Men (4)
1942
1944
1951
1953

Key:
BR—Billingsley Report
CFRA—College Football Researches Association
CSA—College Squash Association
CW—Casper Whitney
HAF—Helms Athletic Foundation
HS—Houlgate System
ICSA—Intercollegiate Sailing Association
IRA—Intercollegiate Rowing Association
NCF—National Championship Foundation
NIWFA—National Intercollegiate Women's Fencing Association
PD—Parke H. Davis
RAAC—Rowing Association of American Colleges

Source: Yale Sports Information Department

CPSIA information can be obtained
at www.ICGtesting.com
Printed in the USA
BVHW051641140722
642163BV00014B/117/J